LEGACY

Created By:
SAM Morrison

LEGACY

Lessons that you teach your family will help create the LEGACY you want to leave.

Use this book to write down your thoughts on the different topics.

Remember more is caught than taught so make sure your actions match your words.

Journaling your thoughts, ideas and beliefs will be good for you and those that you share this book with.

Blessings.

SAM Morrison
SafeHeartConnections.com
CreativeSAMiam.com

ISBN-13:9781514640272
ISBN-10:1514640279

LEGACY

To:

_____

From:

_____

Date: _____

LEGACY

The most important thing is:

_____

_____

_____

_____

_____

_____

_____

_____

_____

_____

_____

_____

_____

_____

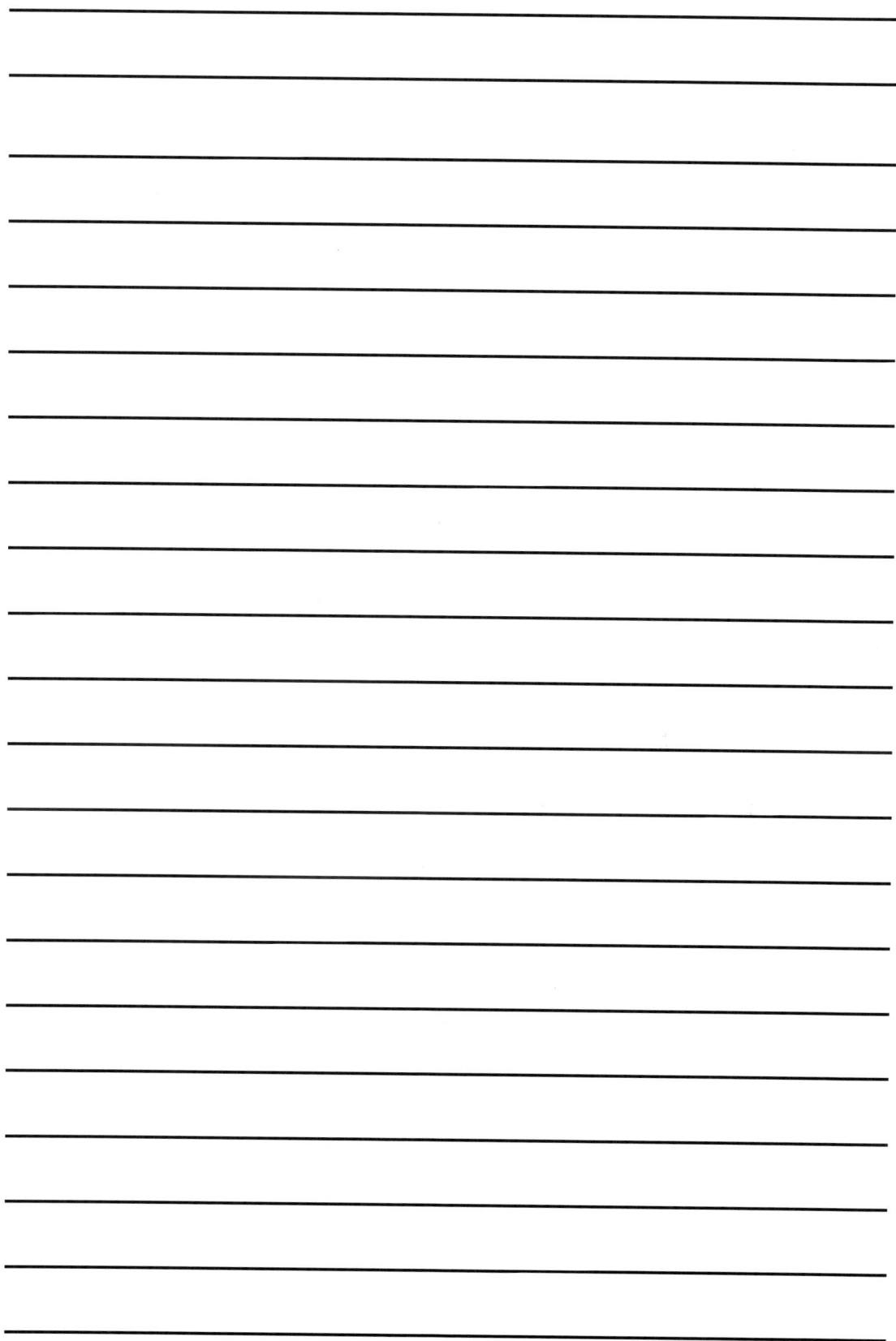

LEGACY

What I believe about love, real love:

_____

_____

_____

_____

_____

_____

_____

_____

_____

_____

_____

_____

_____

_____

_____

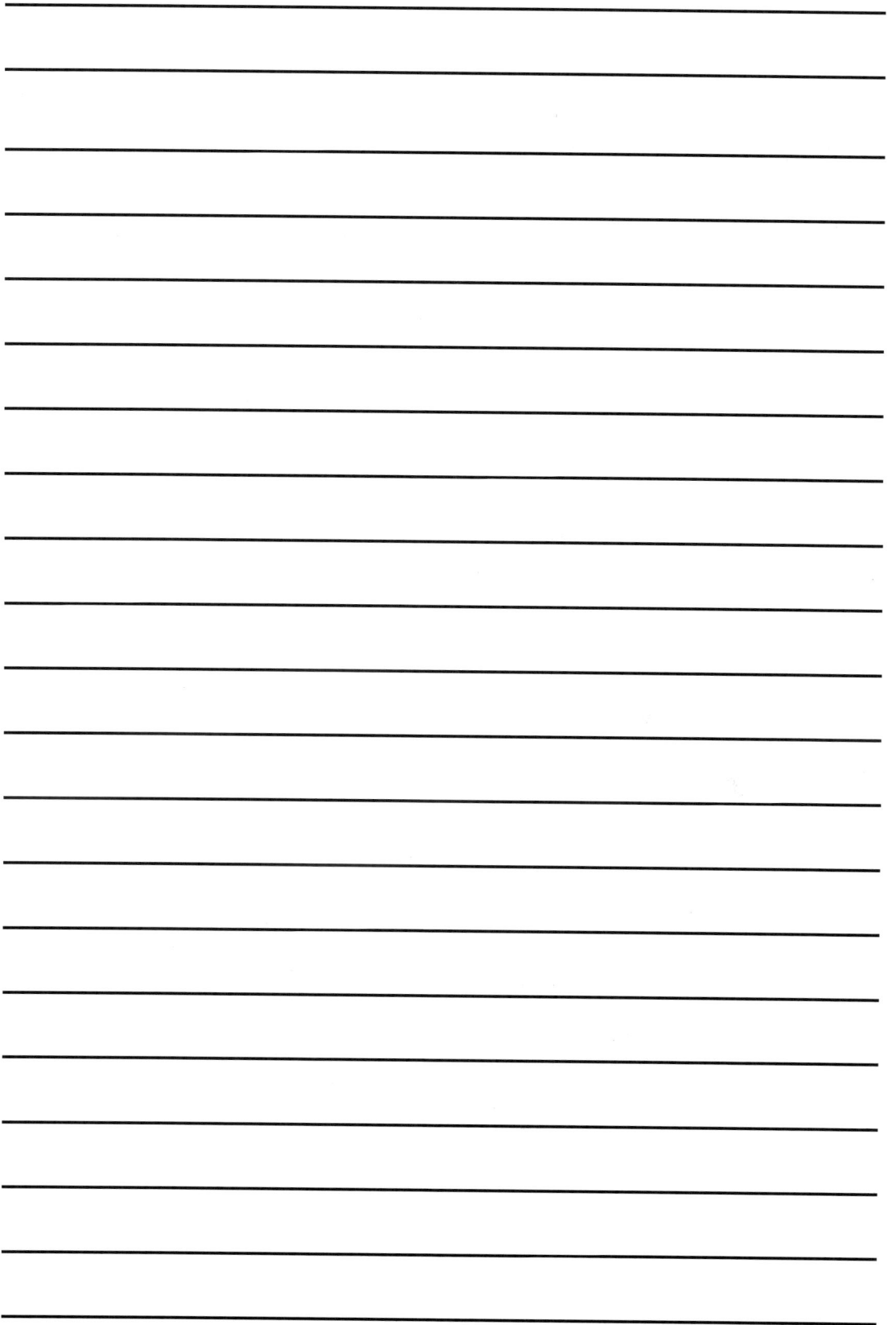

LEGACY

What I believe about God:

_____

_____

_____

_____

_____

_____

_____

_____

_____

_____

_____

_____

_____

_____

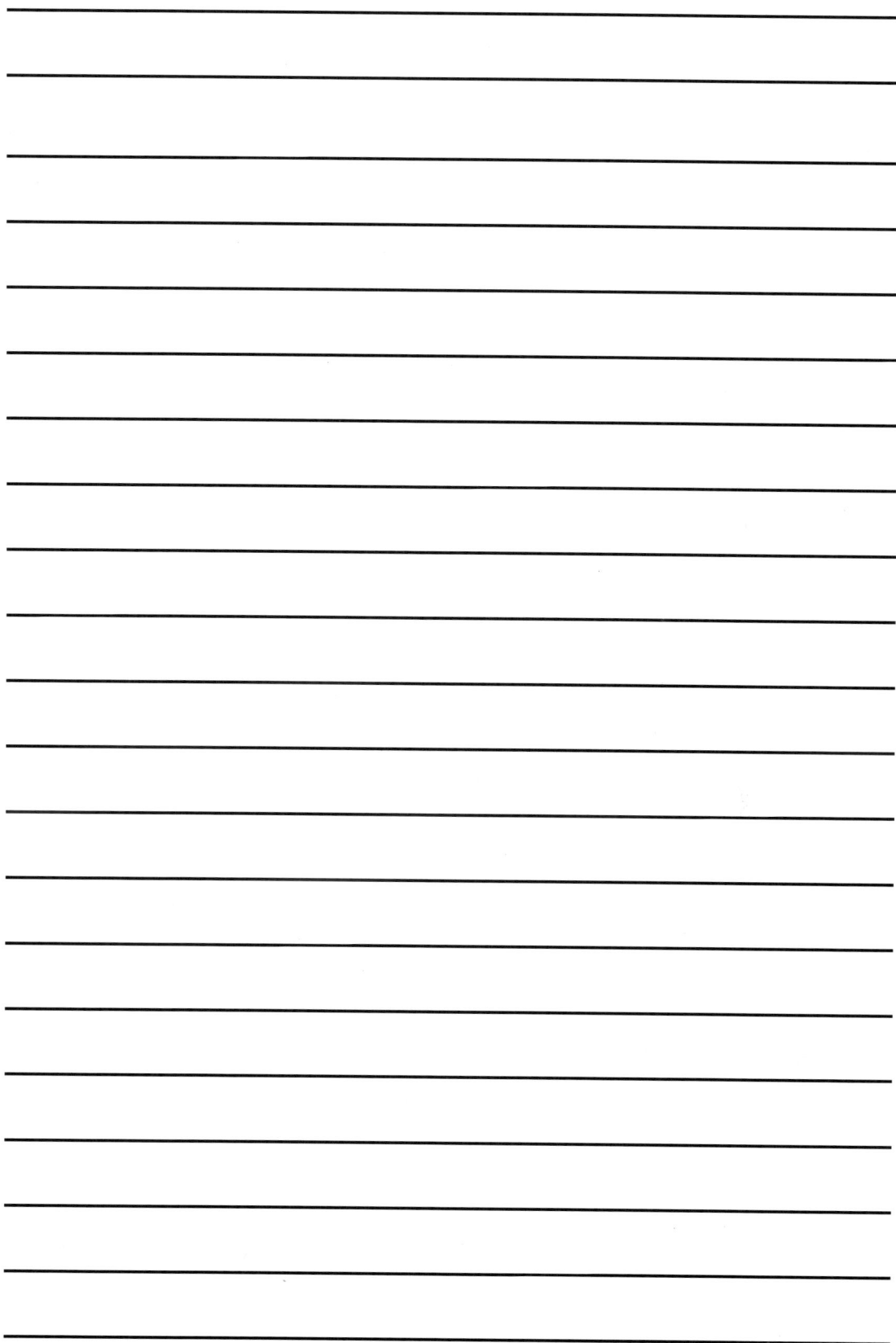

LEGACY

What I believe about friendships:

_____

_____

_____

_____

_____

_____

_____

_____

_____

_____

_____

_____

_____

_____

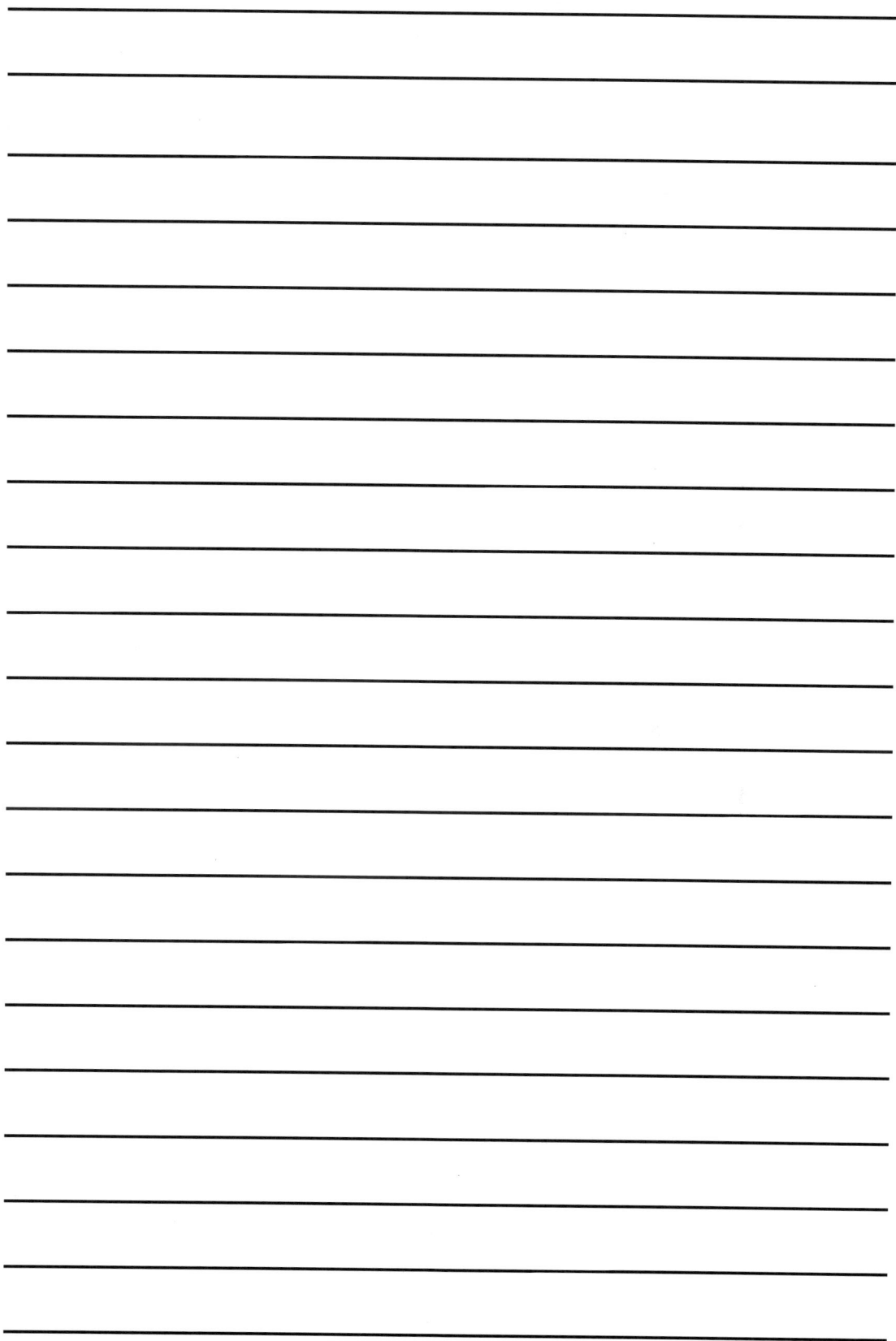

LEGACY

What I believe about loyalty:

_____

_____

_____

_____

_____

_____

_____

_____

_____

_____

_____

_____

_____

_____

_____

_____

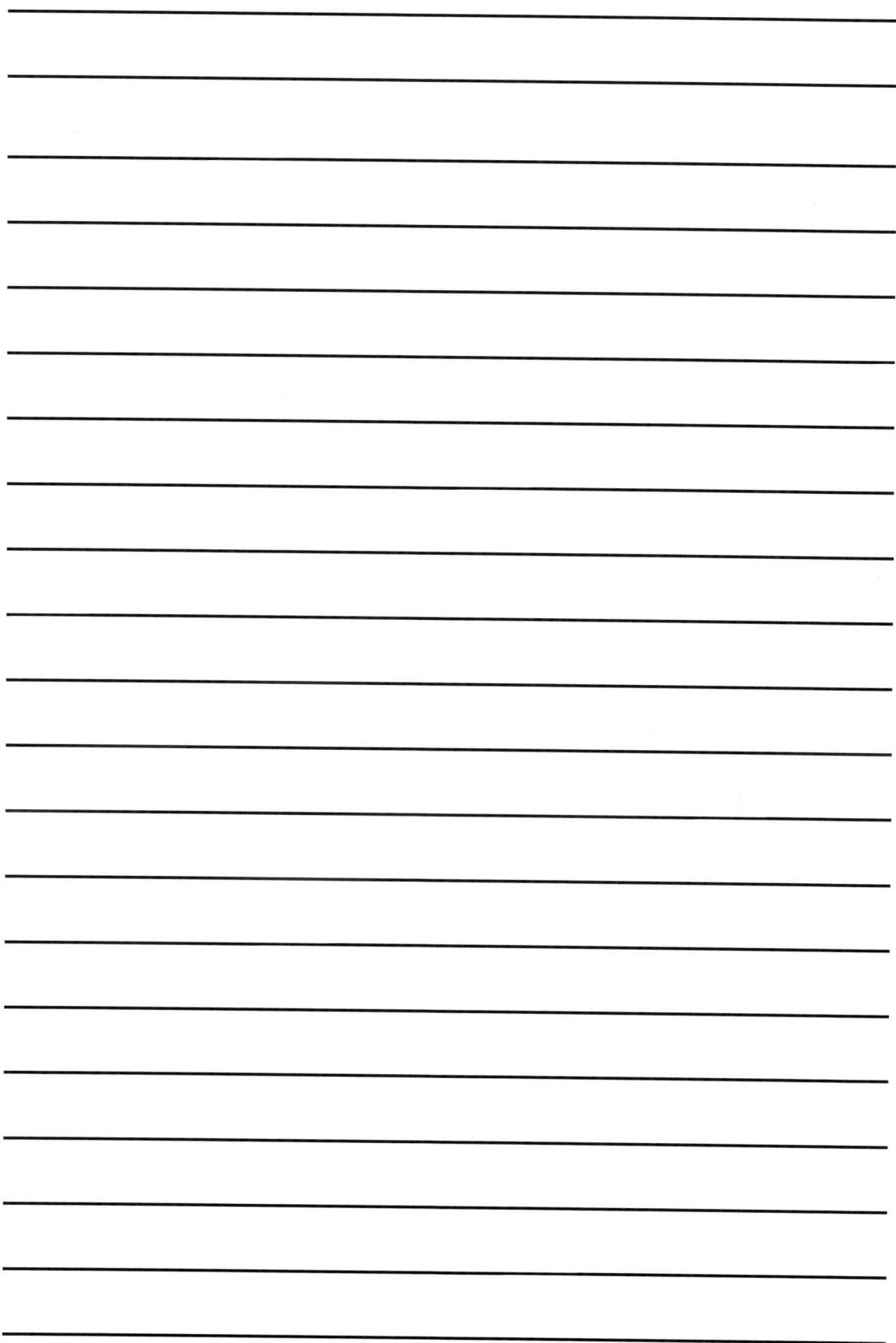

LEGACY

What I believe about honor:

_____

_____

_____

_____

_____

_____

_____

_____

_____

_____

_____

_____

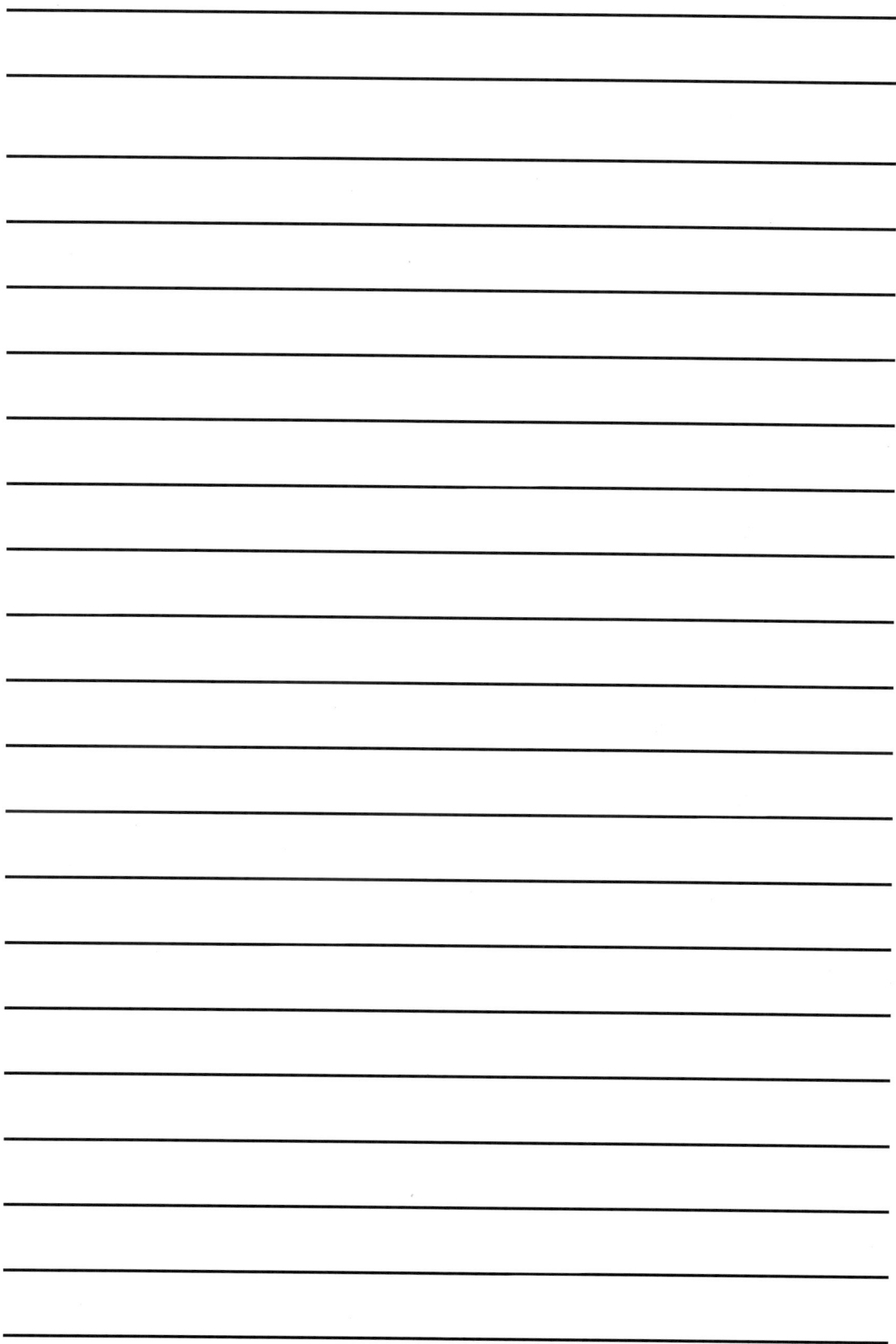

LEGACY

What I believe about integrity:

_____

_____

_____

_____

_____

_____

_____

_____

_____

_____

_____

_____

_____

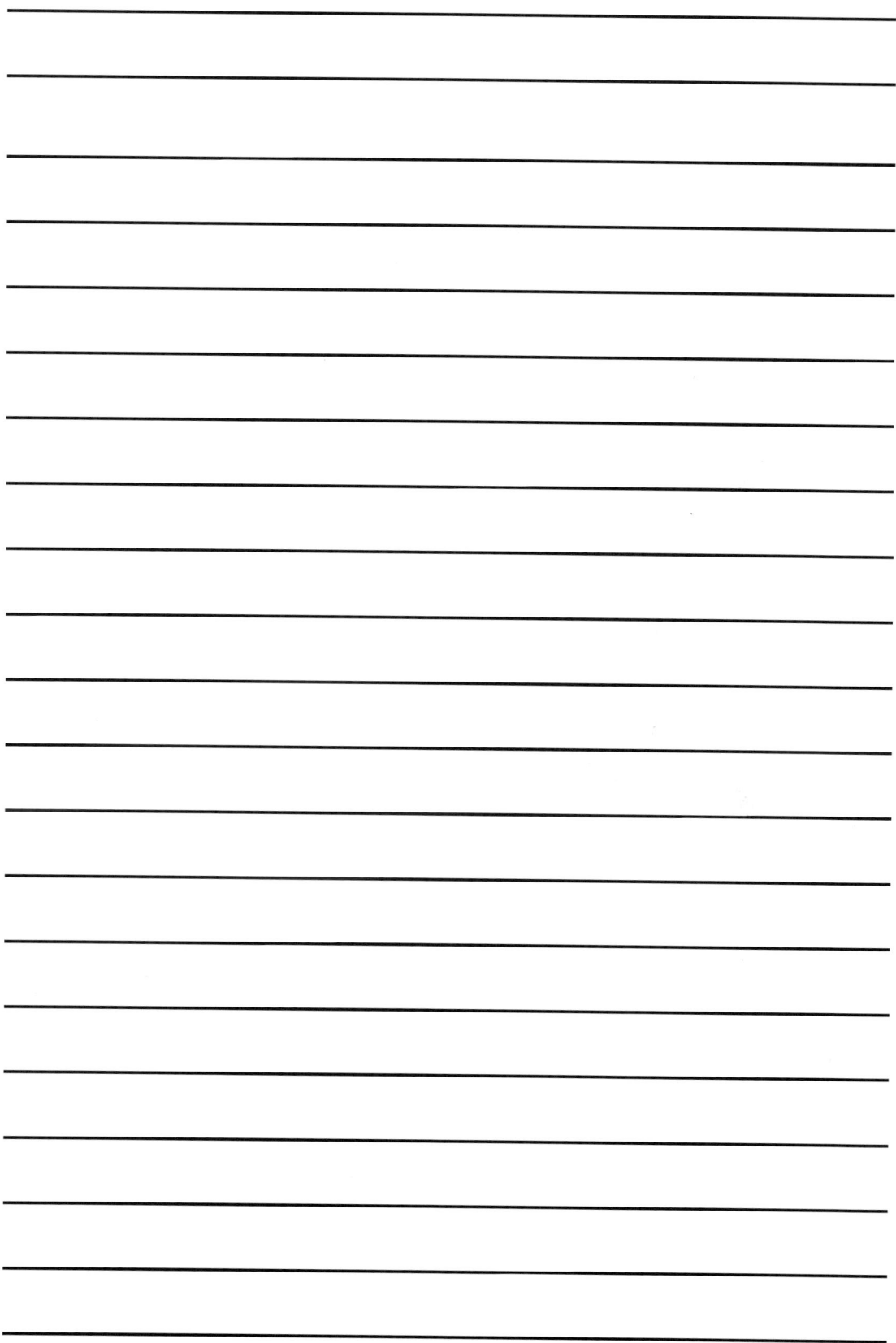

LEGACY

What I believe about money:

_____

_____

_____

_____

_____

_____

_____

_____

_____

_____

_____

_____

_____

_____

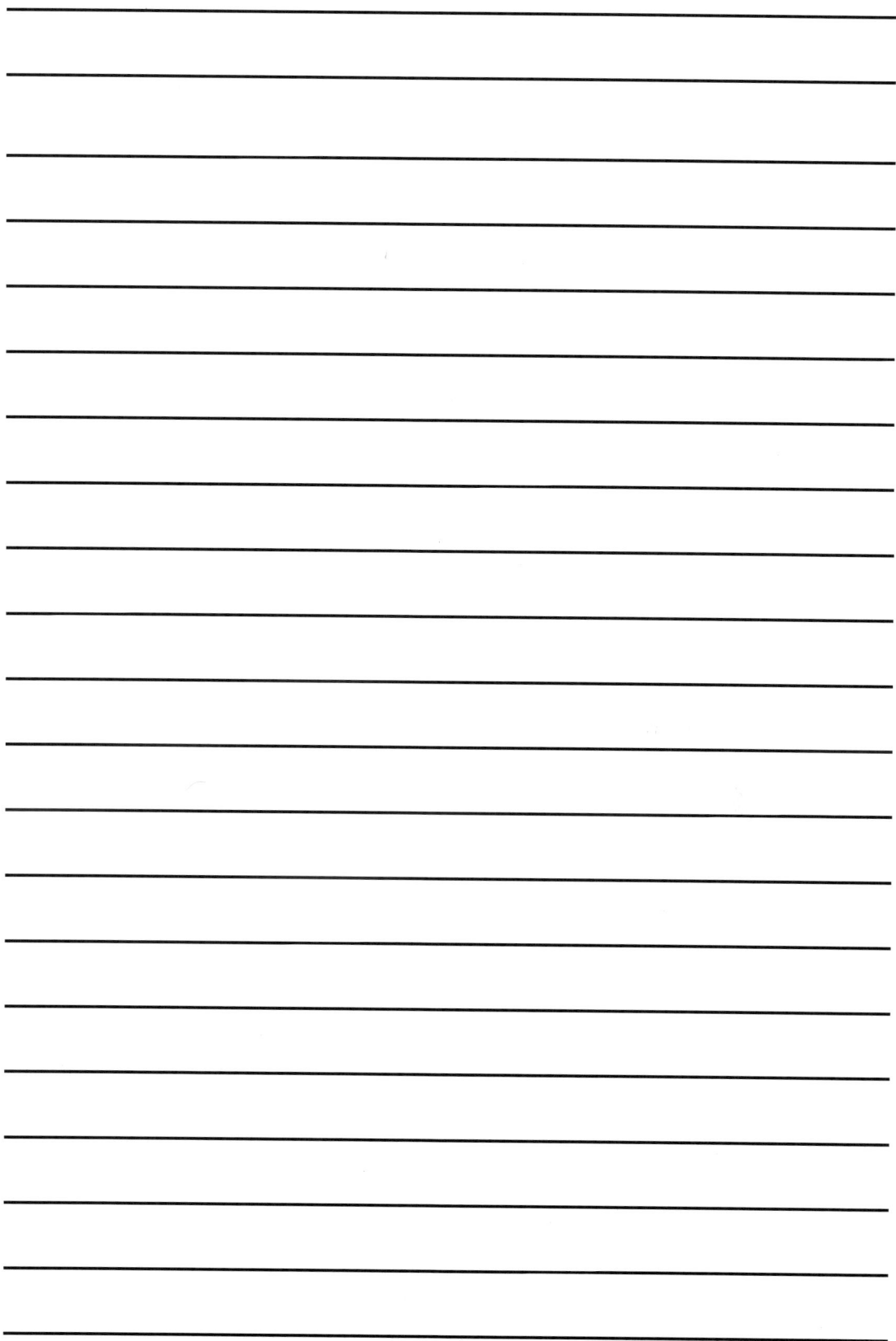

LEGACY

What I believe about serving:

_____

_____

_____

_____

_____

_____

_____

_____

_____

_____

_____

_____

_____

_____

_____

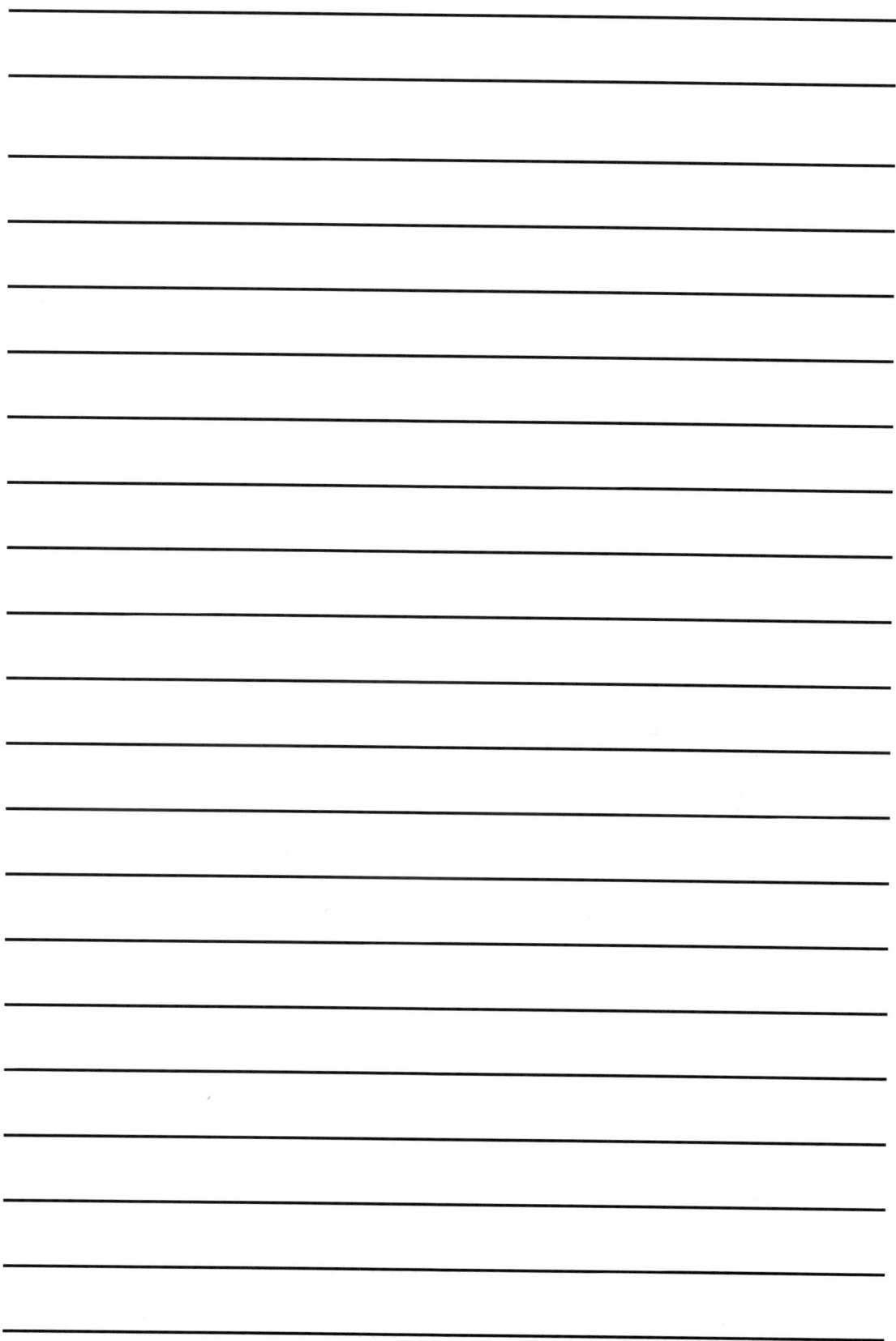

LEGACY

What I believe about grace:

_____

_____

_____

_____

_____

_____

_____

_____

_____

_____

_____

_____

_____

_____

_____

_____

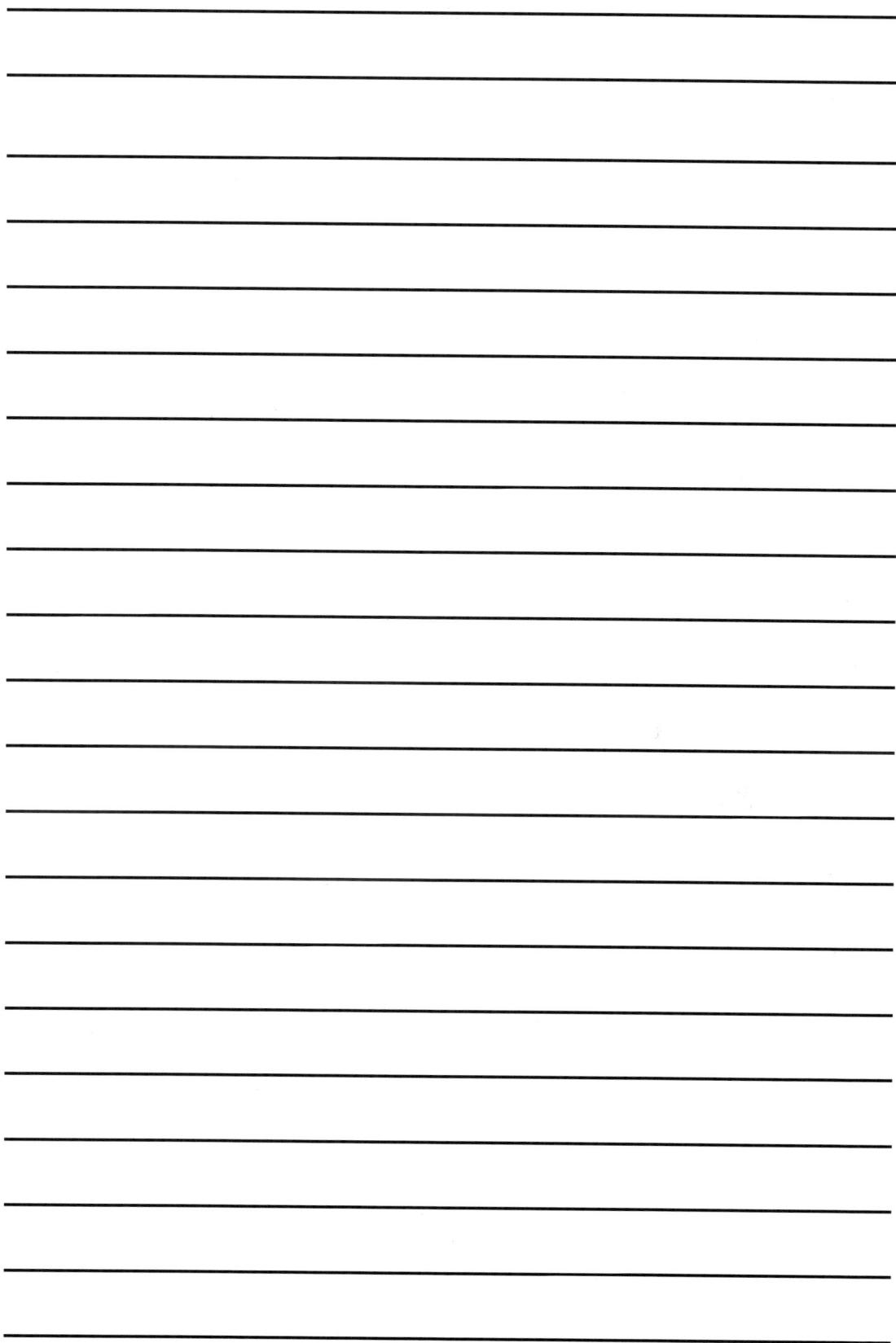

LEGACY

What I believe about forgiveness:

_____

_____

_____

_____

_____

_____

_____

_____

_____

_____

_____

_____

_____

_____

_____

_____

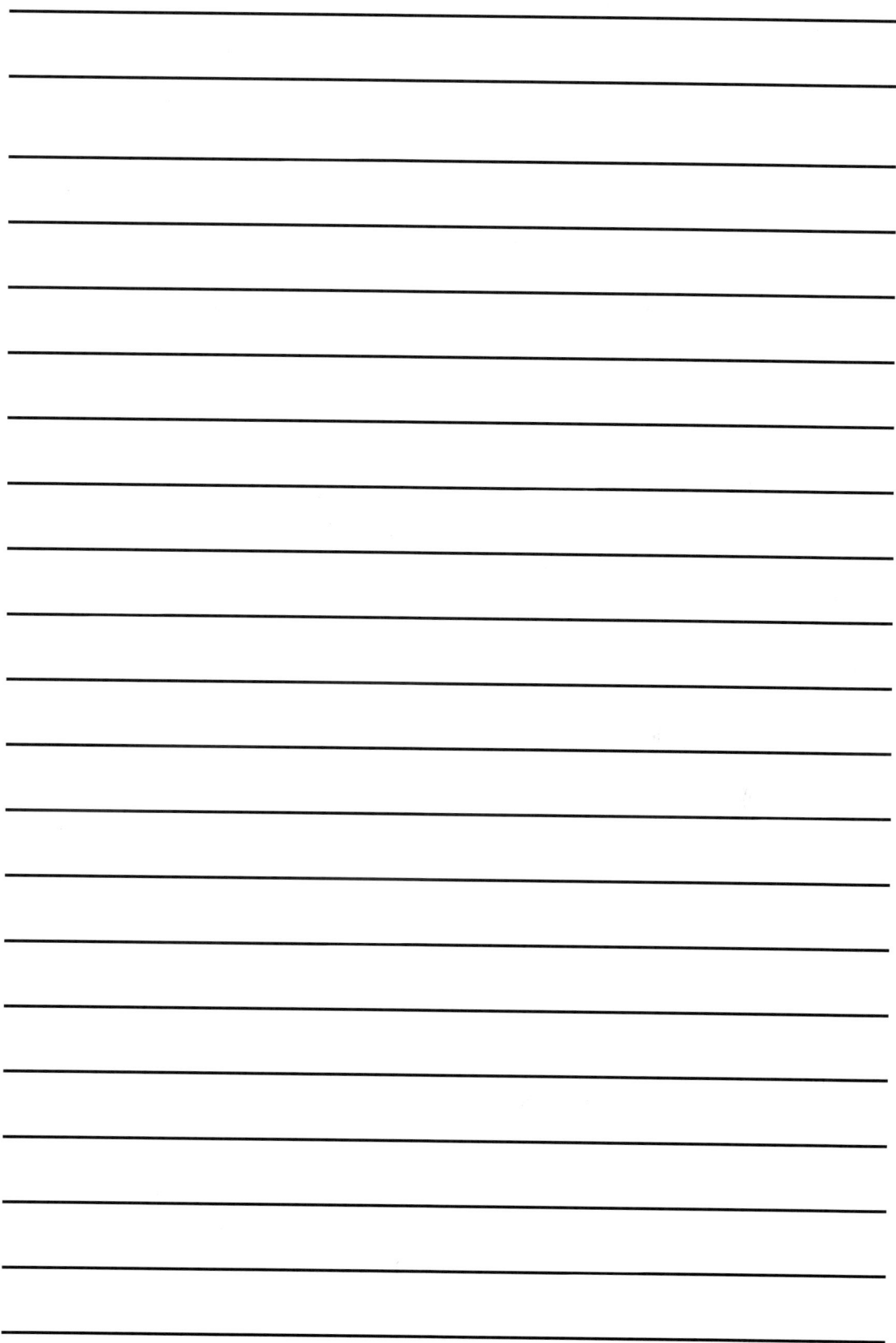

LEGACY

What I believe about mentorship:

_____

_____

_____

_____

_____

_____

_____

_____

_____

_____

_____

_____

_____

_____

_____

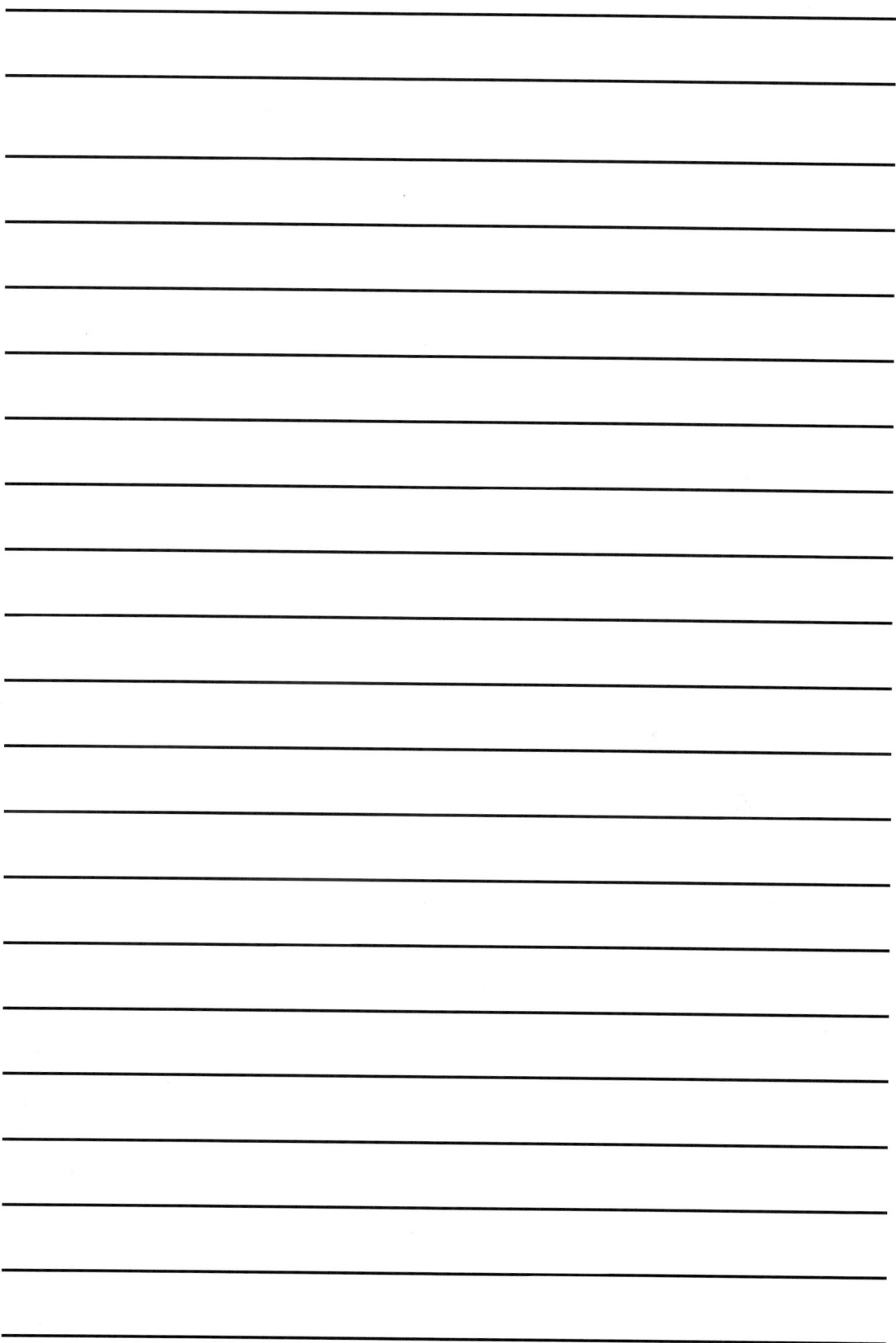

LEGACY

What I believe about keeping your promises:

_____

_____

_____

_____

_____

_____

_____

_____

_____

_____

_____

_____

_____

_____

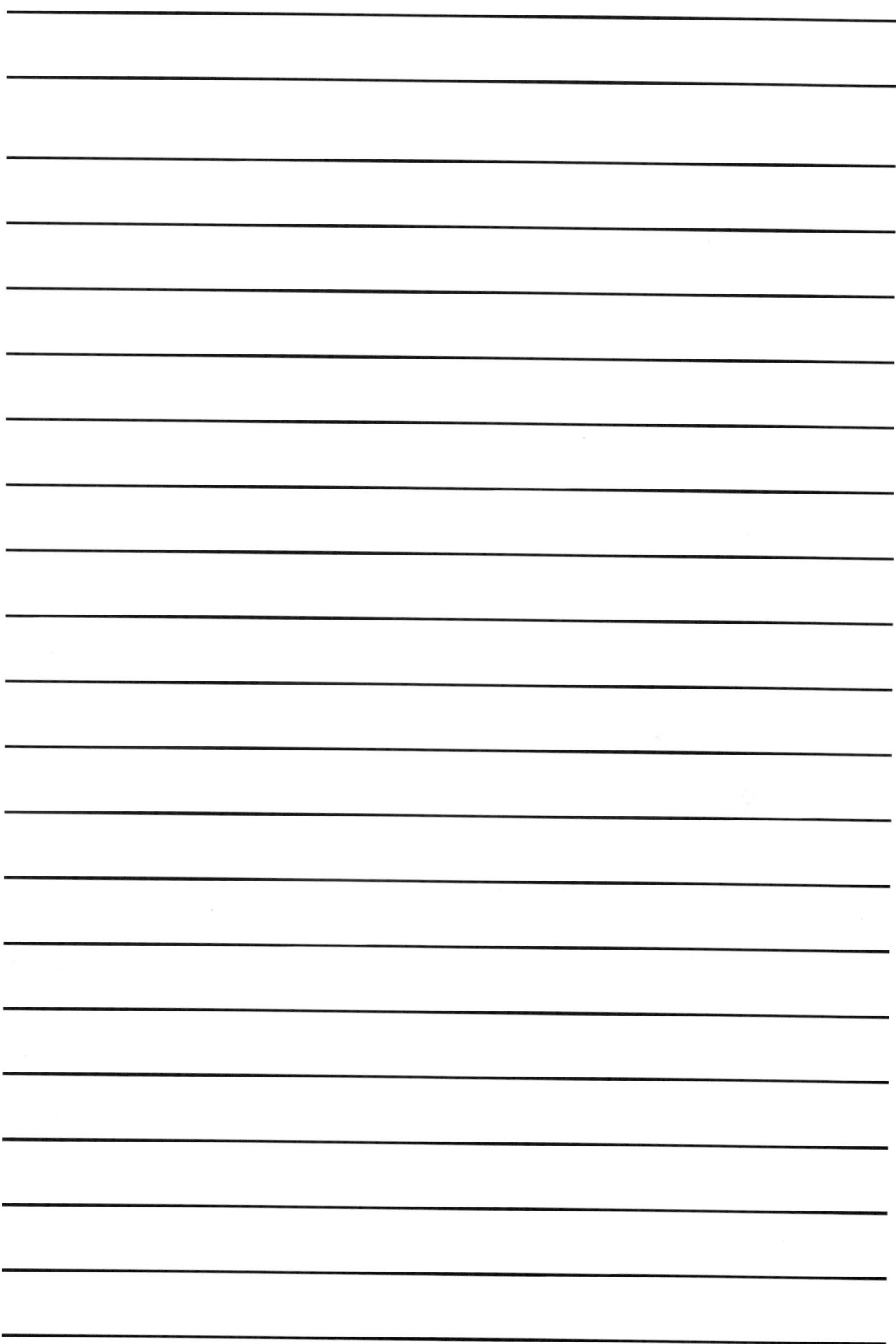

LEGACY

What I believe about strength:

_____

_____

_____

_____

_____

_____

_____

_____

_____

_____

_____

_____

_____

_____

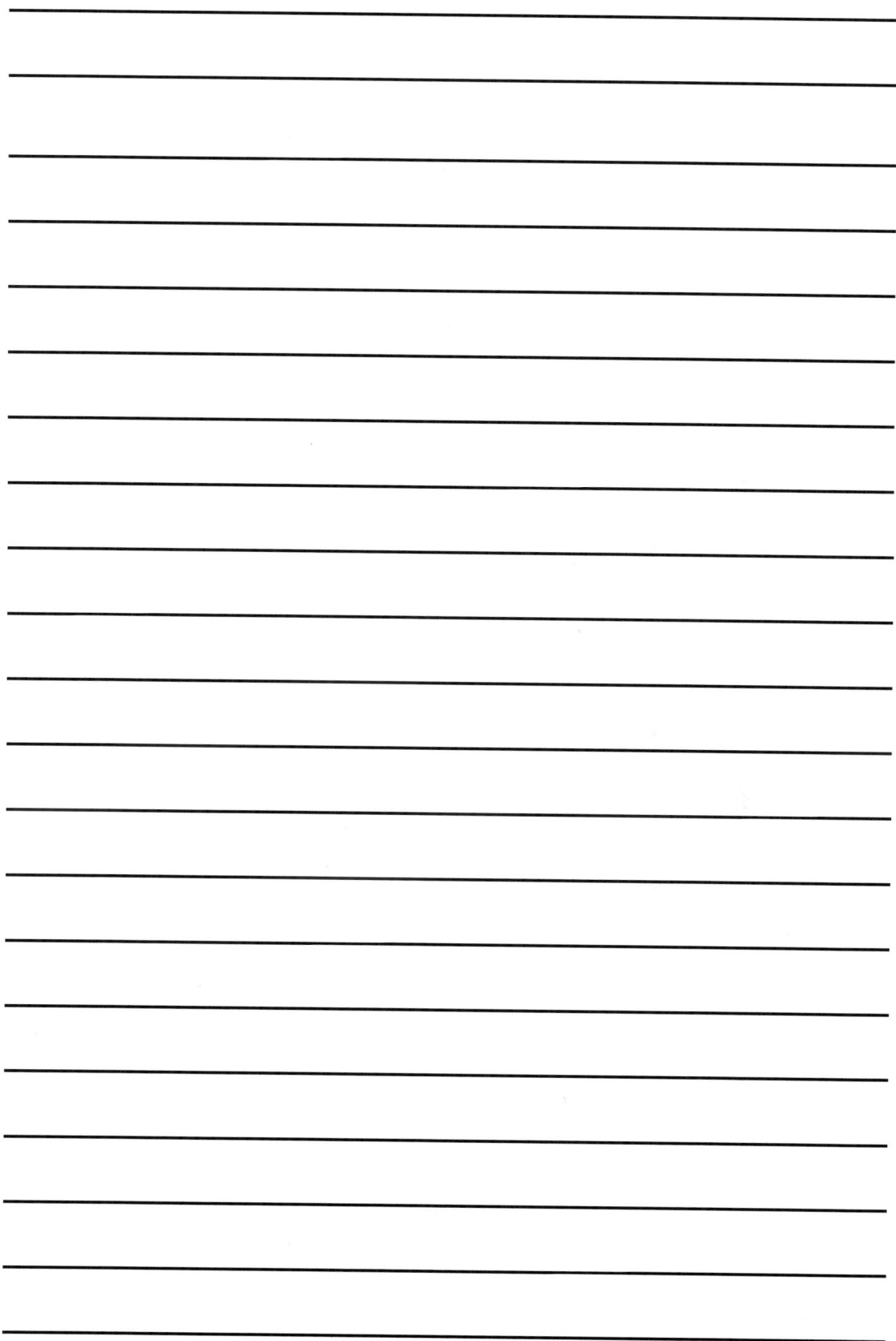

LEGACY

What I believe about power:

_____

_____

_____

_____

_____

_____

_____

_____

_____

_____

_____

_____

_____

_____

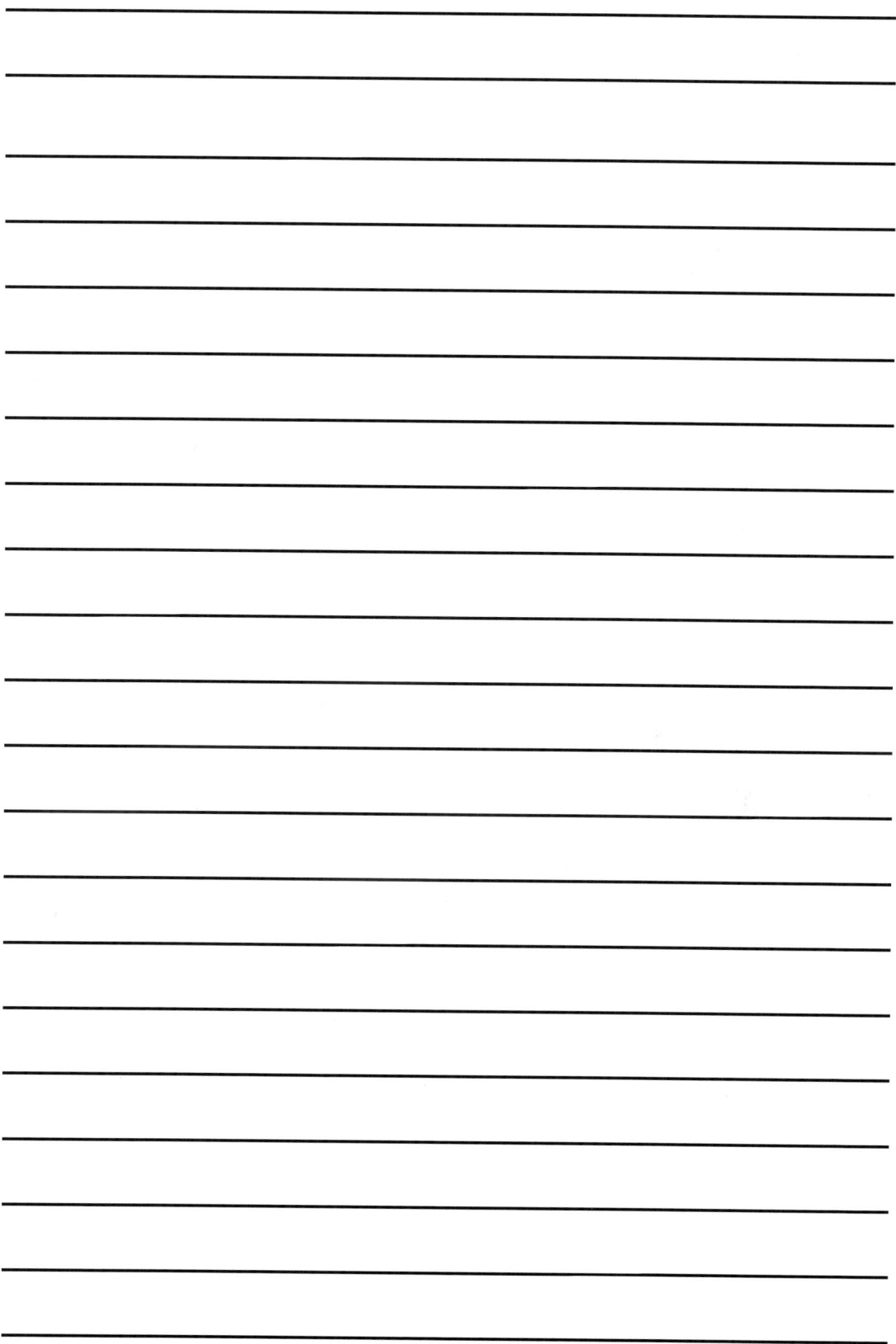

LEGACY

What I believe about grief:

_____

_____

_____

_____

_____

_____

_____

_____

_____

_____

_____

_____

_____

_____

_____

_____

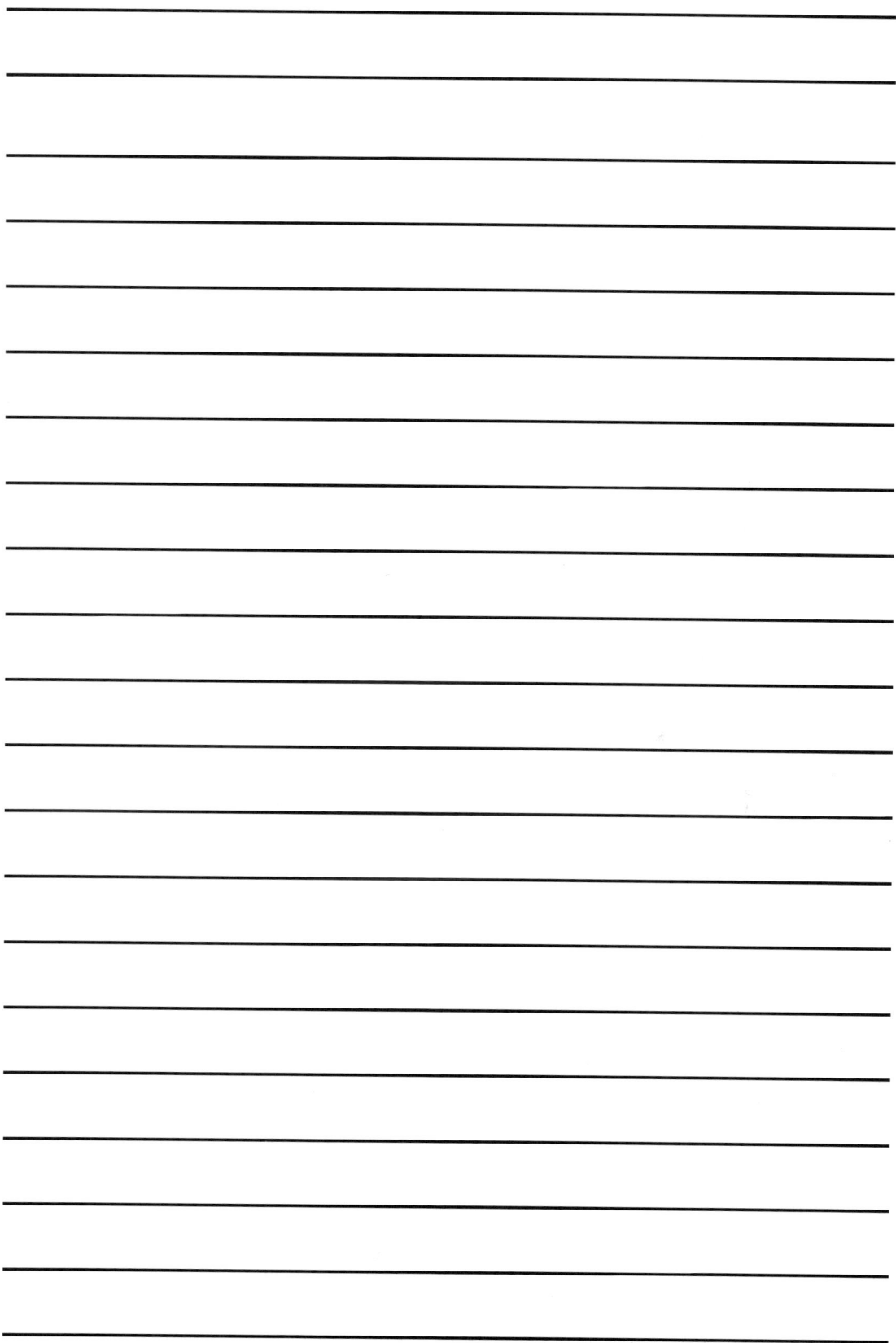

LEGACY

What I believe about authority:

_____

_____

_____

_____

_____

_____

_____

_____

_____

_____

_____

_____

_____

_____

_____

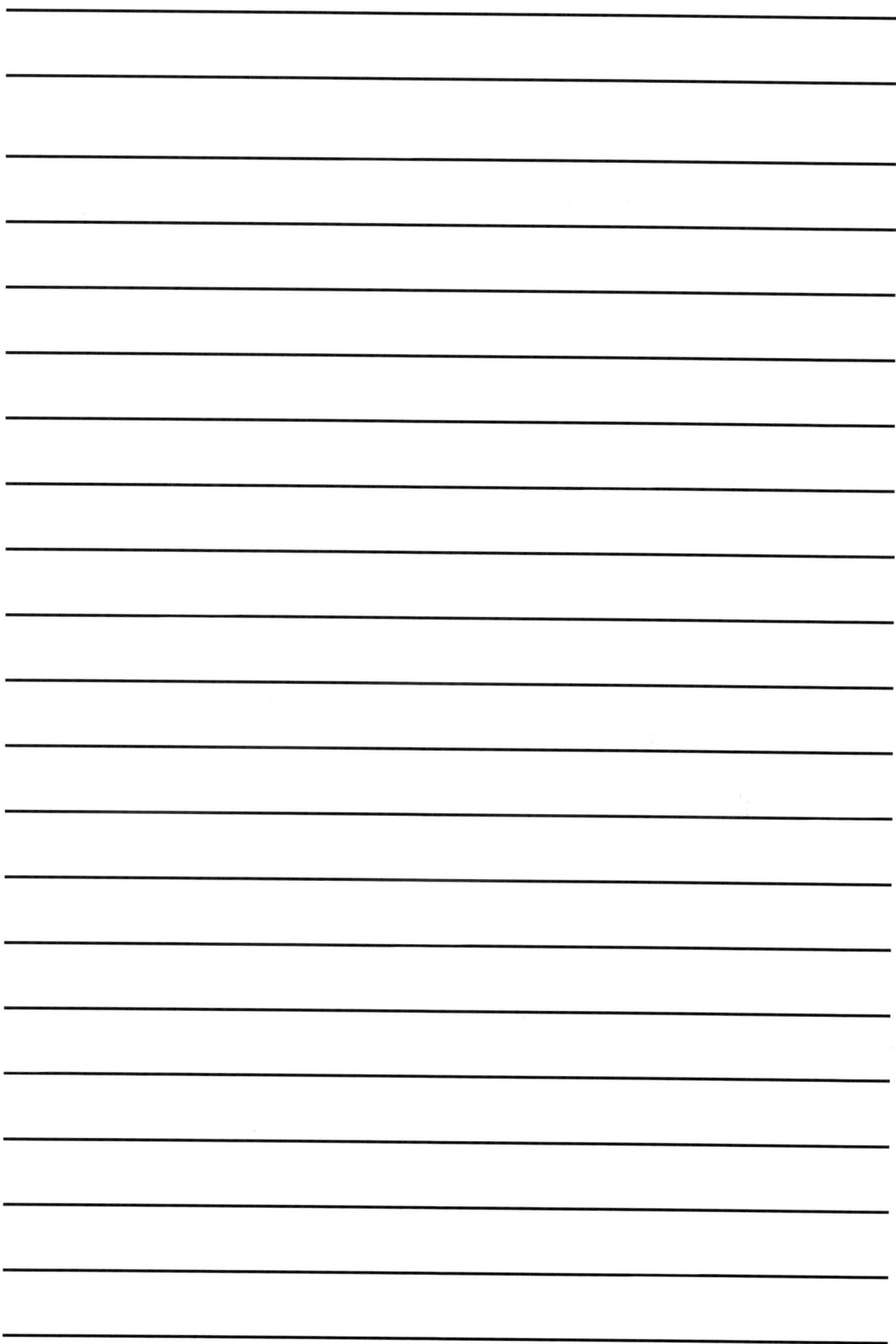

LEGACY

What I believe about trust:

_____

_____

_____

_____

_____

_____

_____

_____

_____

_____

_____

_____

_____

_____

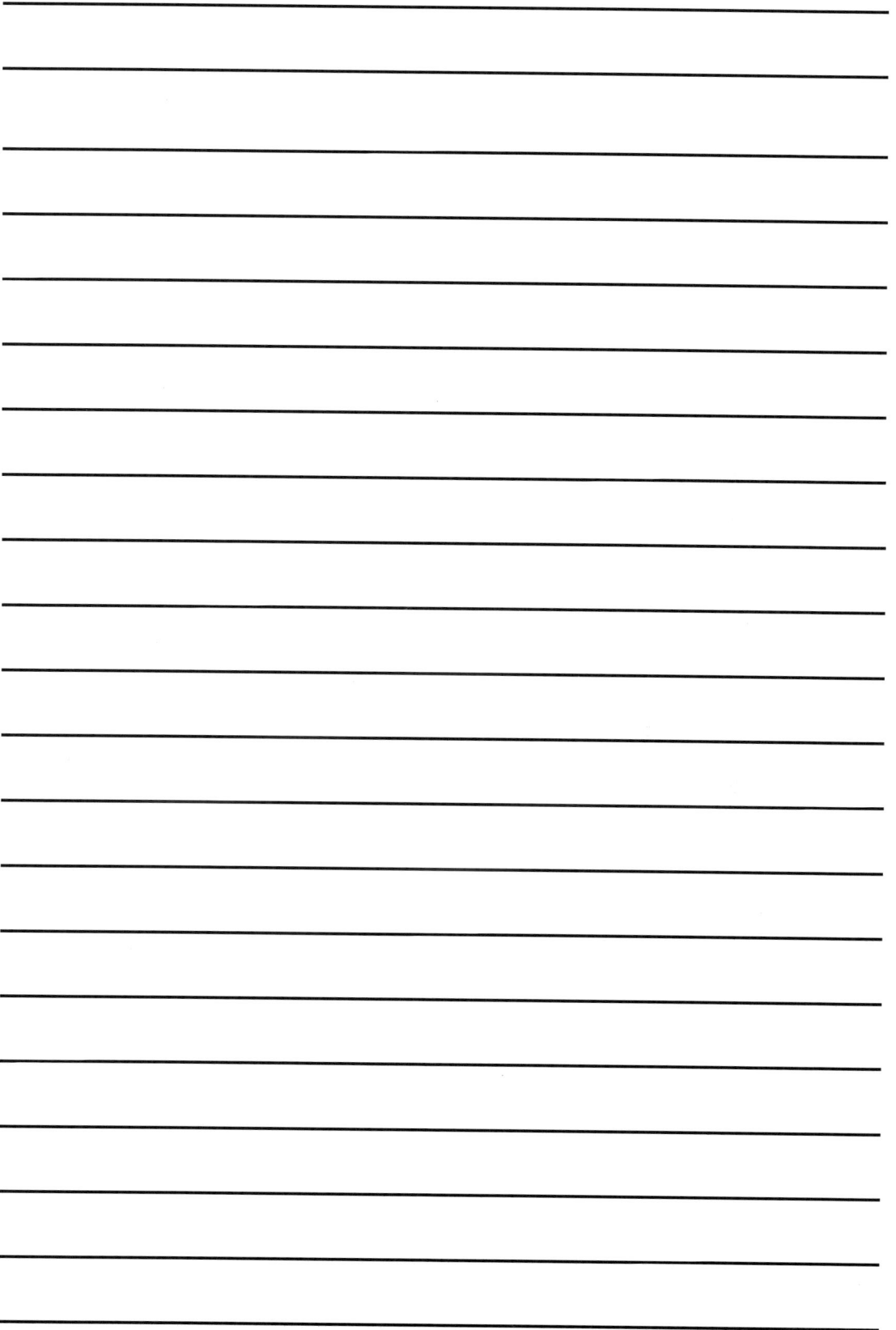

LEGACY

What I believe about giving thanks:

_____

_____

_____

_____

_____

_____

_____

_____

_____

_____

_____

_____

_____

_____

_____

_____

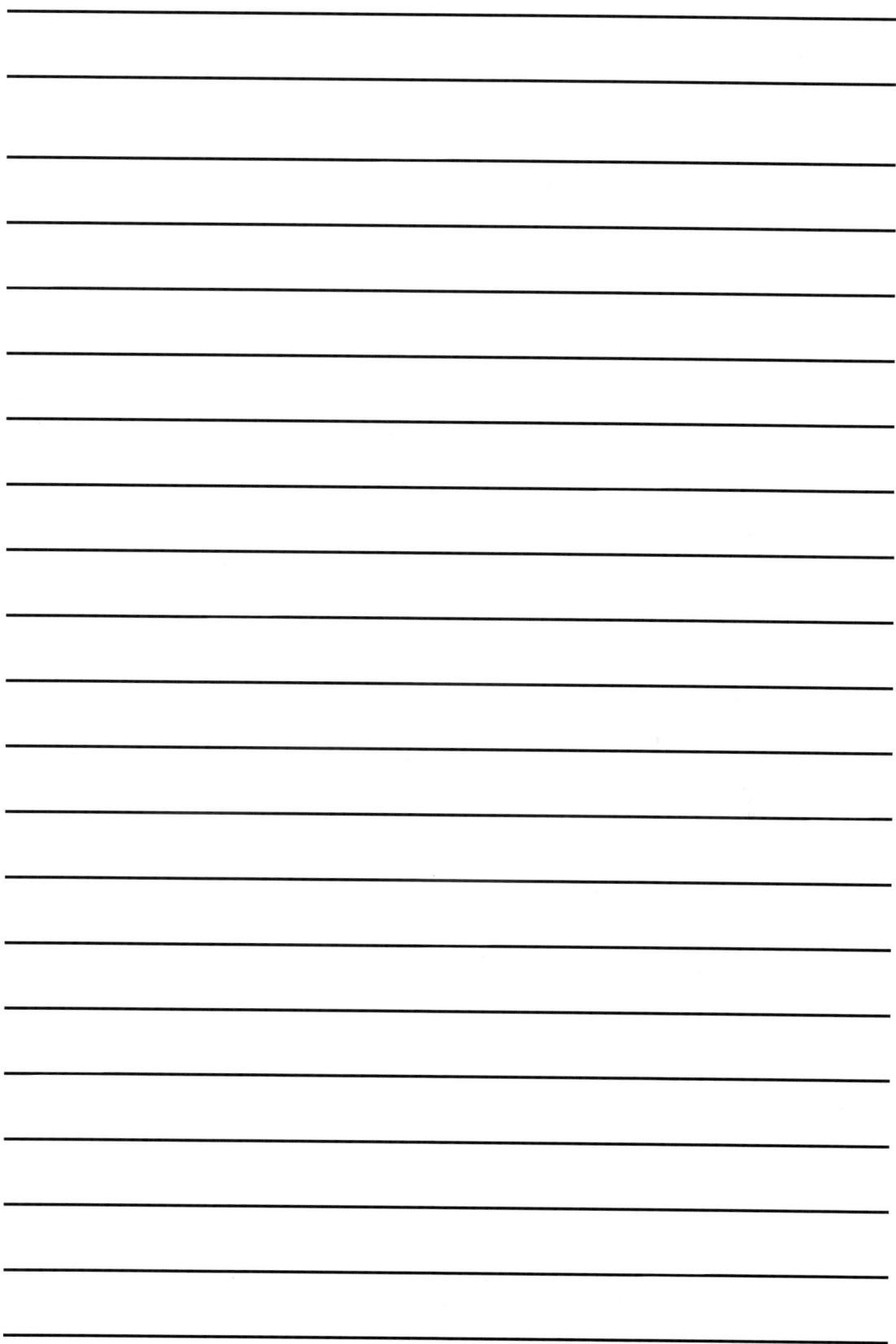

LEGACY

What I believe about work ethics:

_____

_____

_____

_____

_____

_____

_____

_____

_____

_____

_____

_____

_____

_____

_____

_____

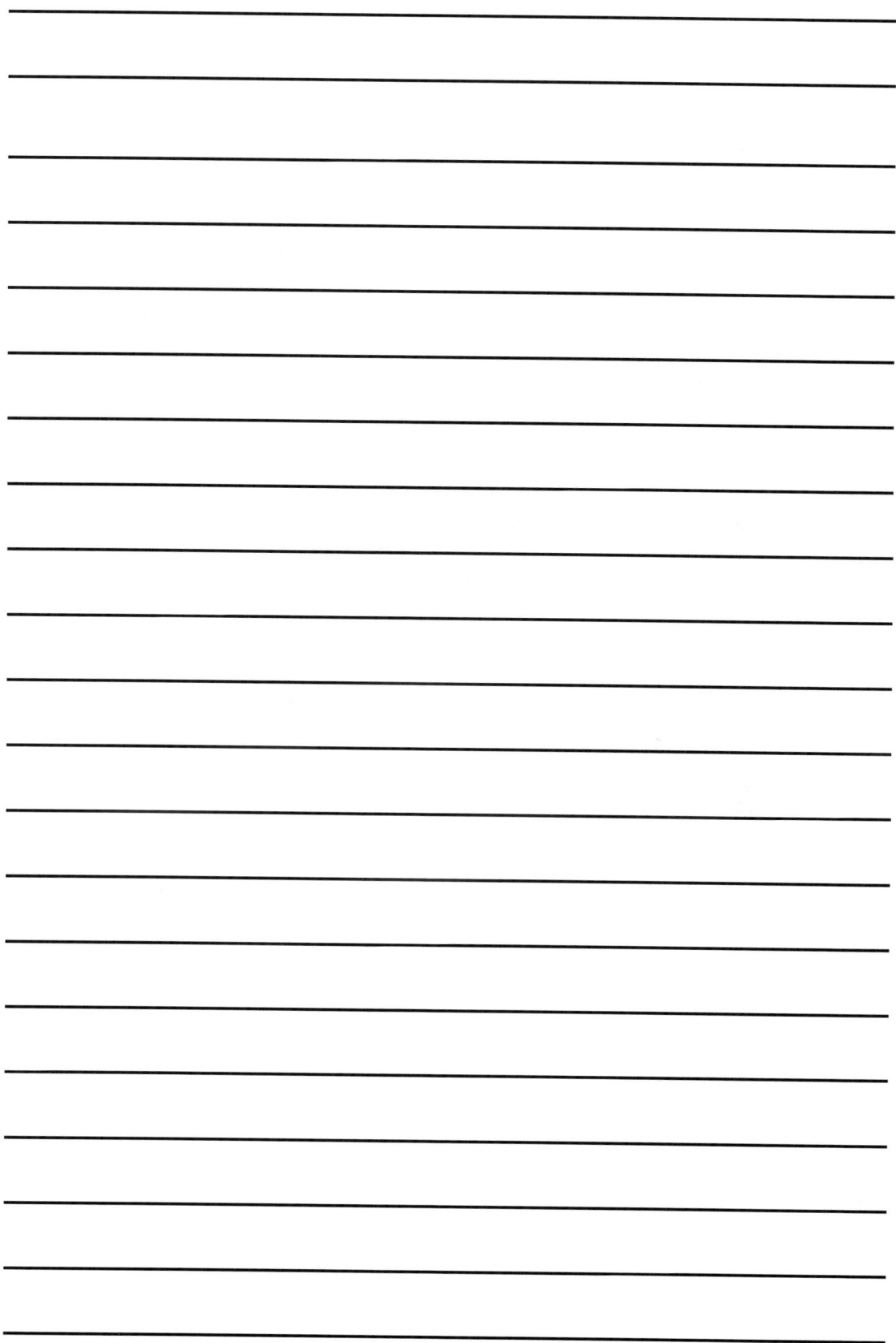

LEGACY

What I believe about failure:

_____

_____

_____

_____

_____

_____

_____

_____

_____

_____

_____

_____

_____

_____

_____

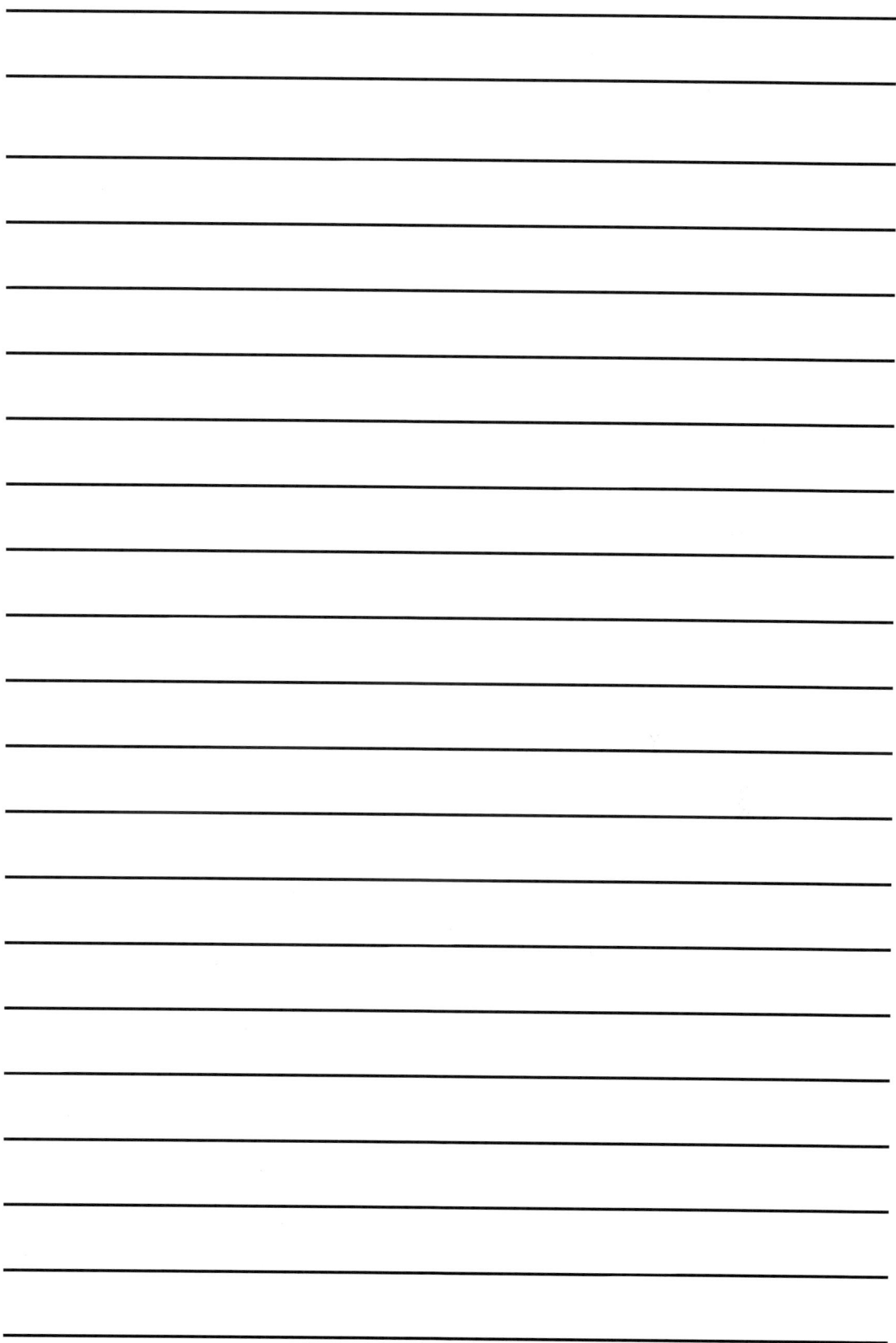

LEGACY

What I believe about respect:

_____

_____

_____

_____

_____

_____

_____

_____

_____

_____

_____

_____

_____

_____

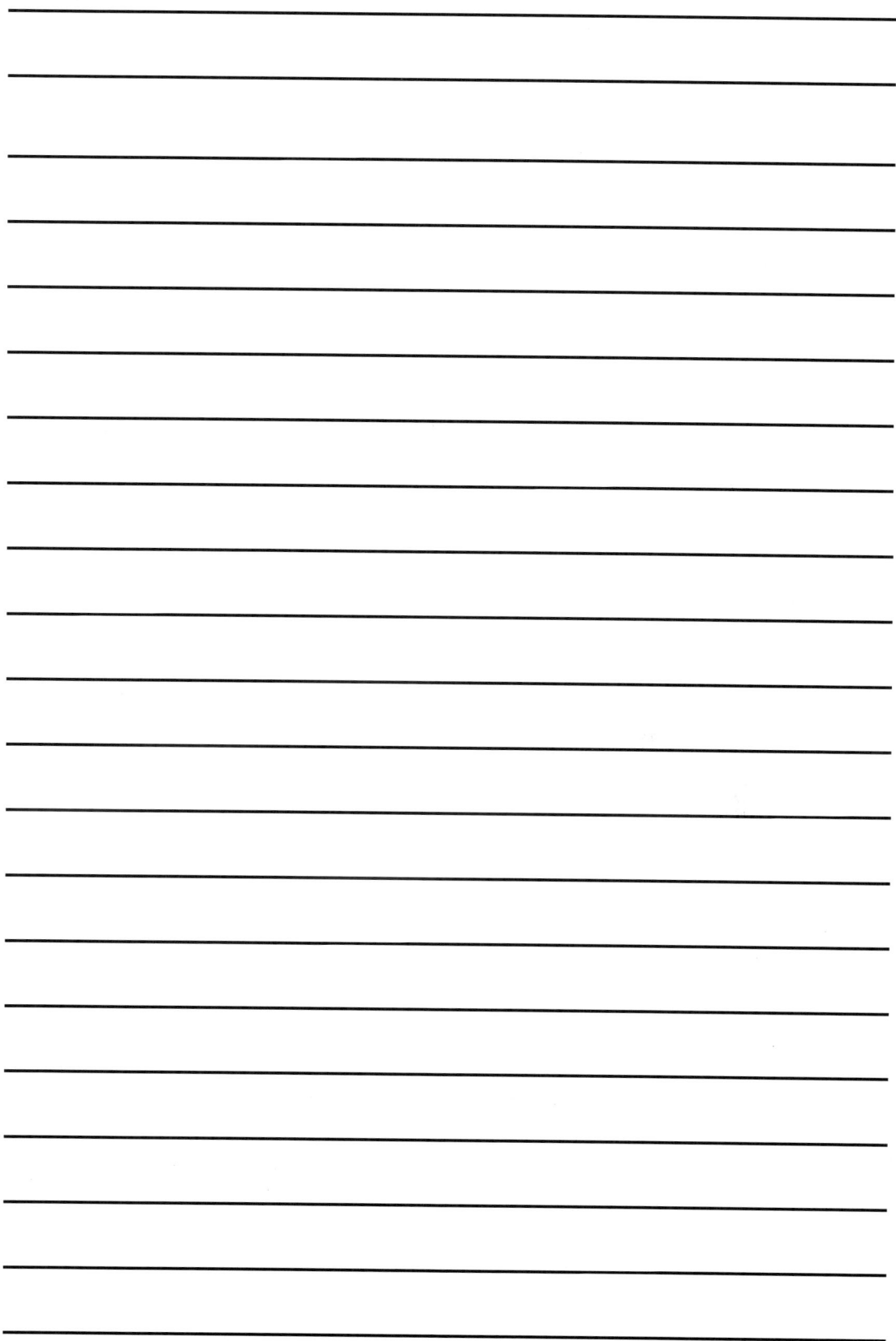

LEGACY

What I believe about natural consequences:

_____

_____

_____

_____

_____

_____

_____

_____

_____

_____

_____

_____

_____

_____

_____

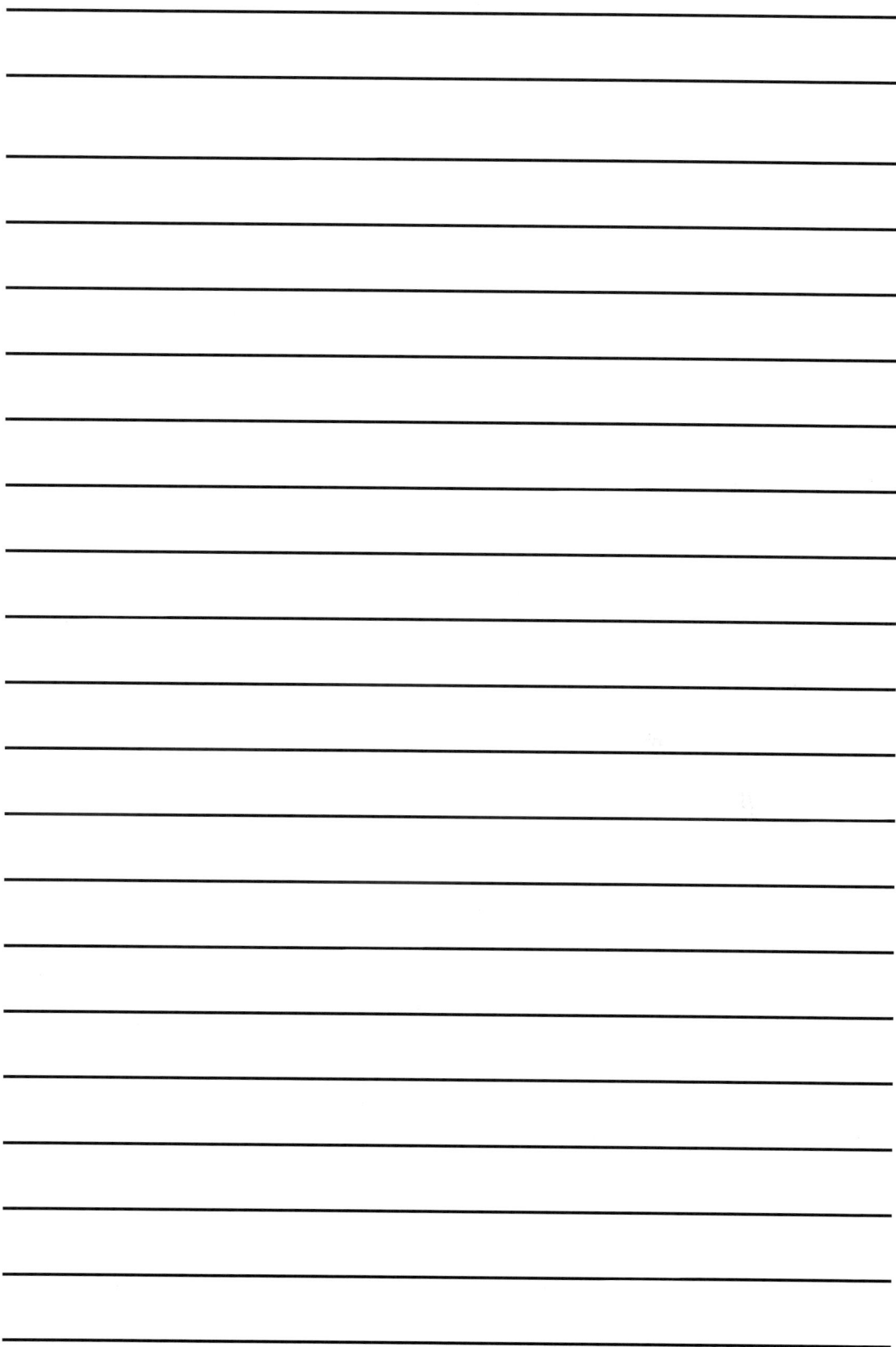

LEGACY

What I believe about gossip:

_____

_____

_____

_____

_____

_____

_____

_____

_____

_____

_____

_____

_____

_____

_____

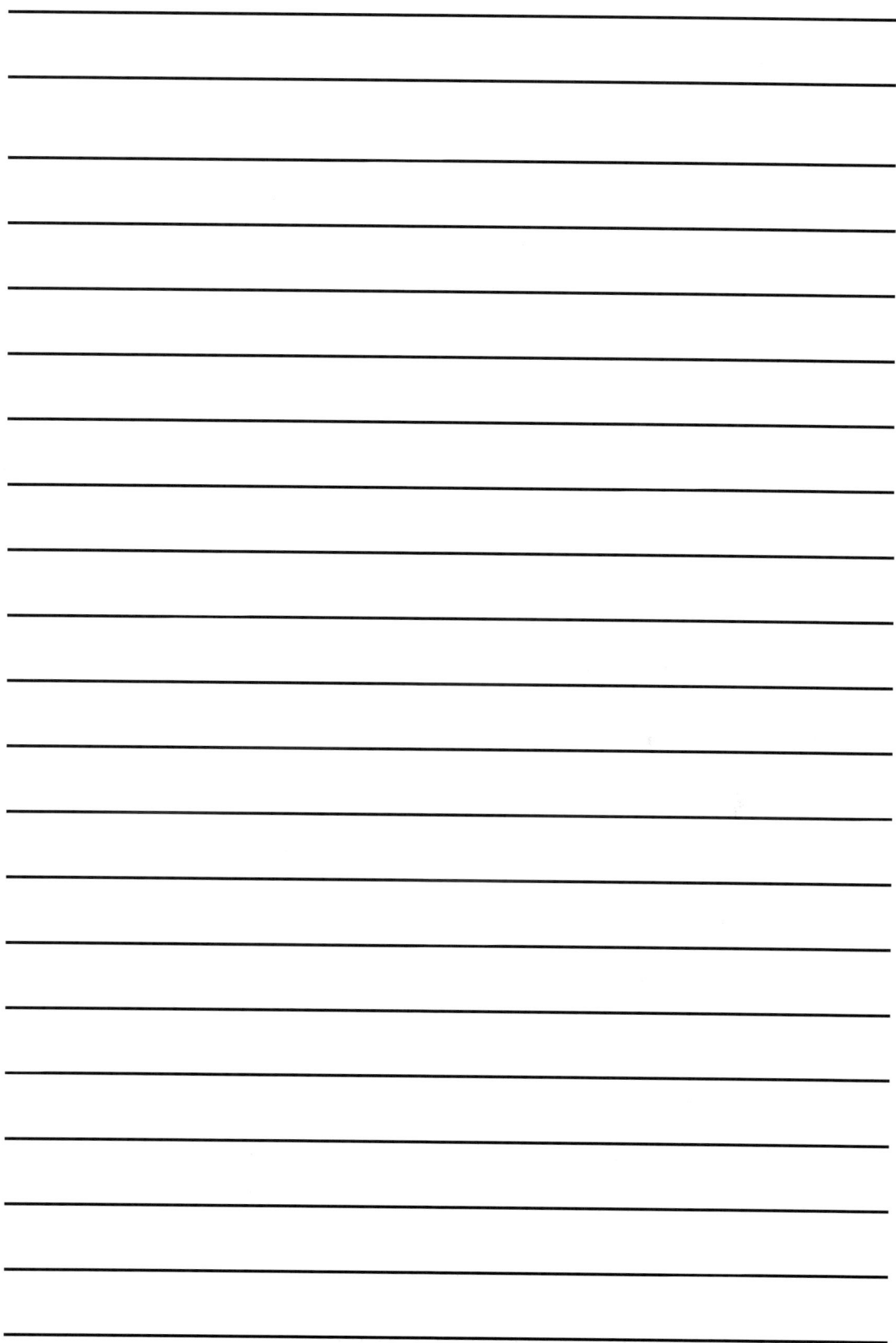

LEGACY

What I believe about marriage:

_____

_____

_____

_____

_____

_____

_____

_____

_____

_____

_____

_____

_____

_____

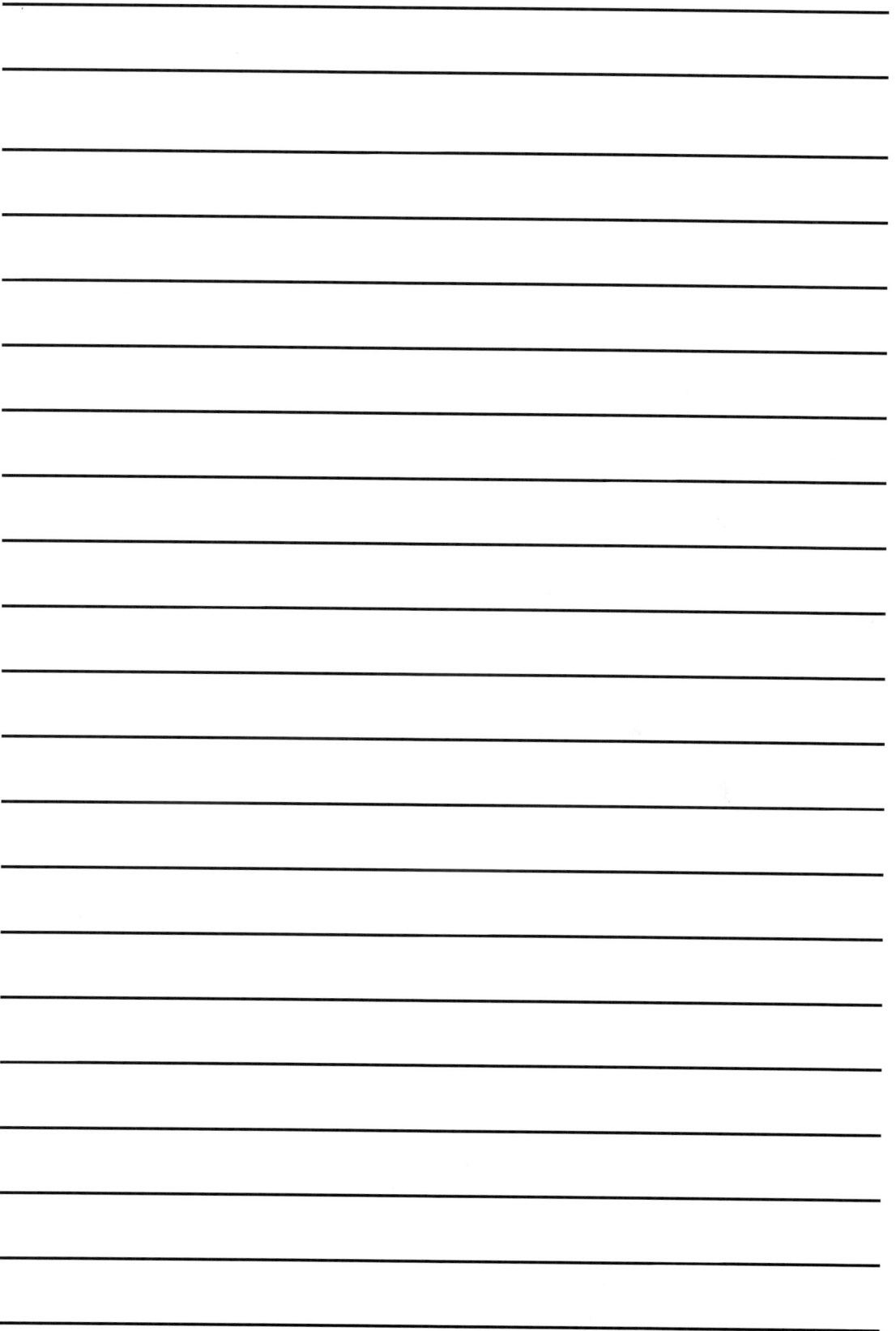

LEGACY

What I believe about sex:

_____

_____

_____

_____

_____

_____

_____

_____

_____

_____

_____

_____

_____

_____

_____

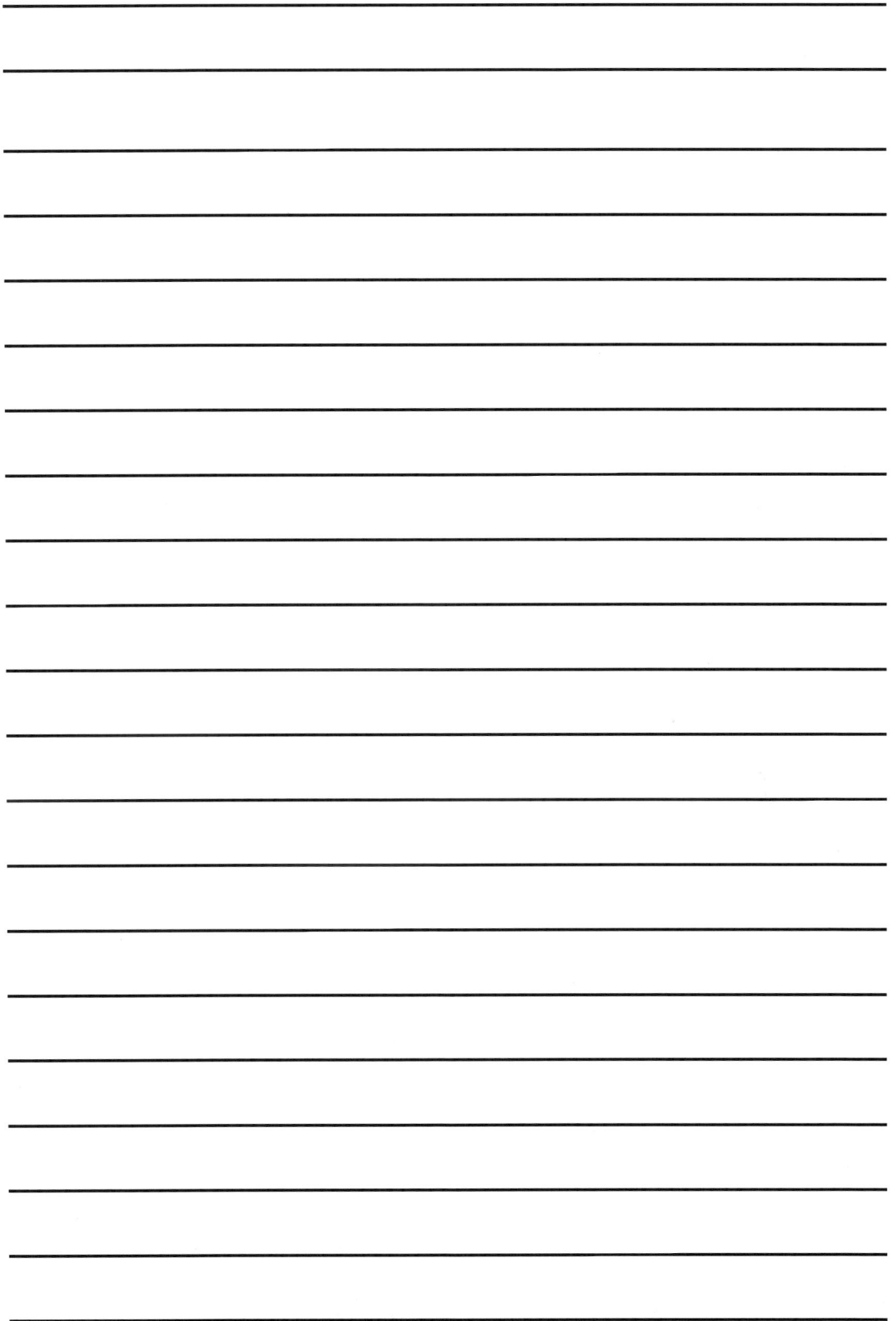

LEGACY

What I believe about addiction:

_____

_____

_____

_____

_____

_____

_____

_____

_____

_____

_____

_____

_____

_____

_____

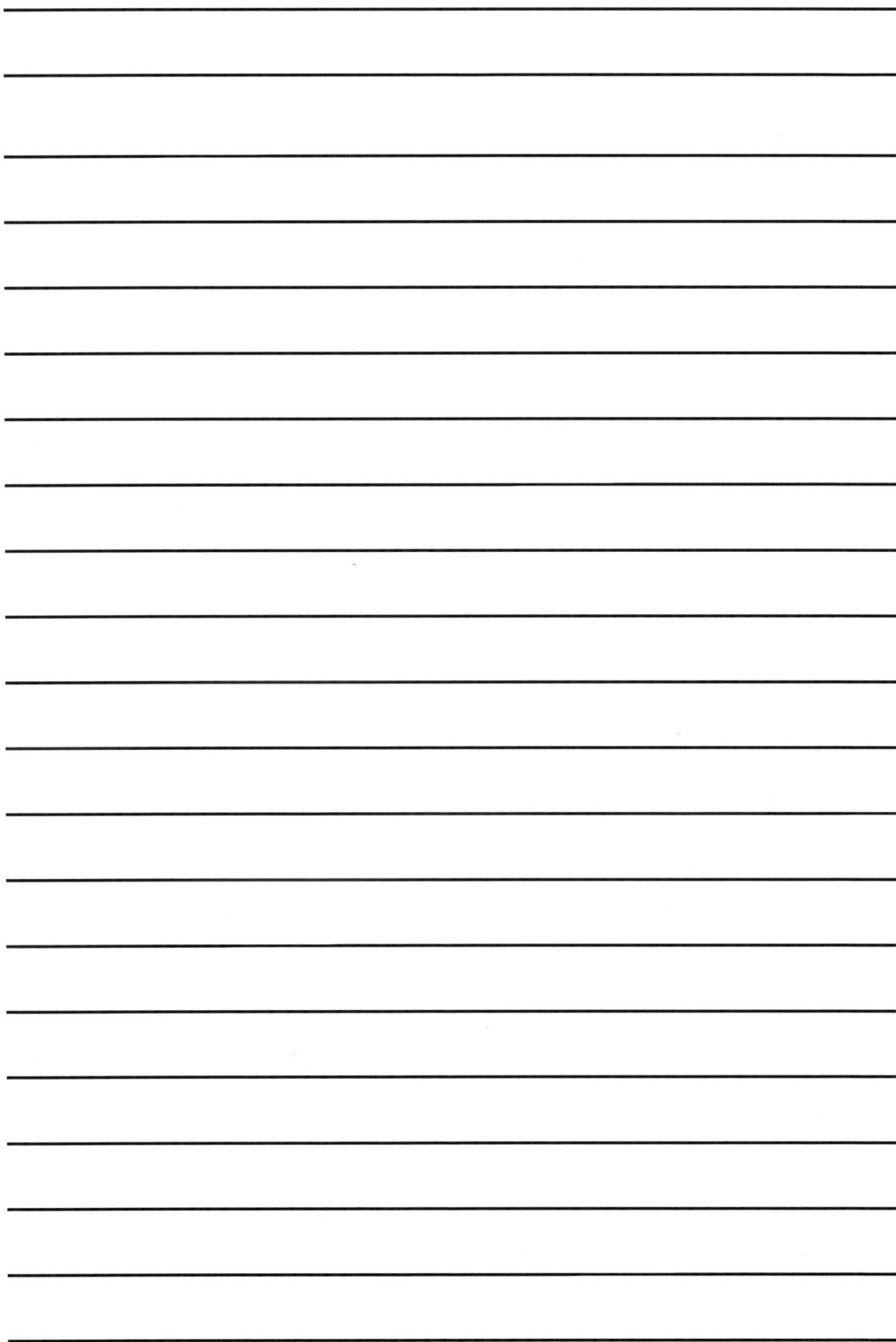

LEGACY

What I believe about education:

_____

_____

_____

_____

_____

_____

_____

_____

_____

_____

_____

_____

_____

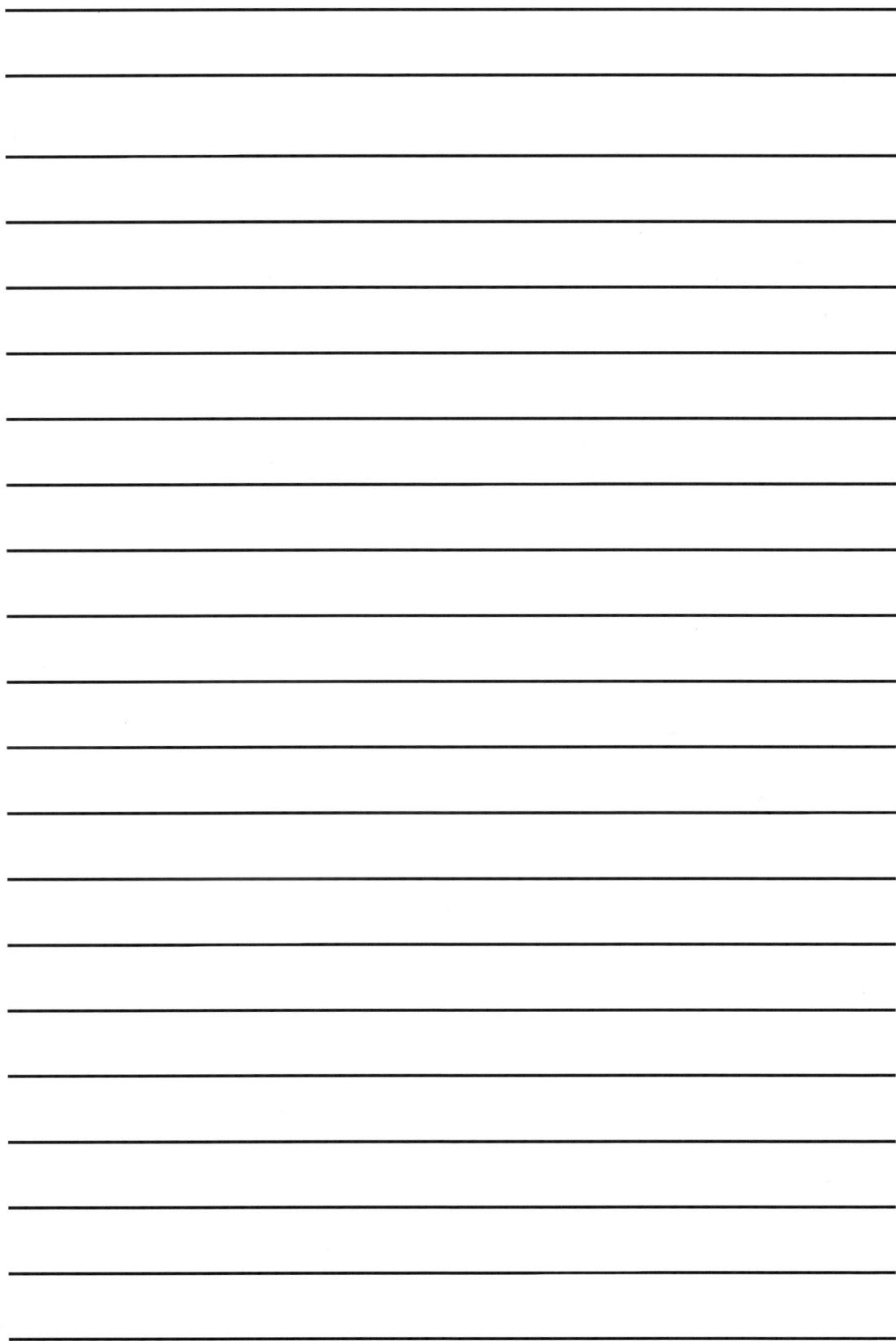

LEGACY

What I believe about boundaries:

_____

_____

_____

_____

_____

_____

_____

_____

_____

_____

_____

_____

_____

_____

_____

_____

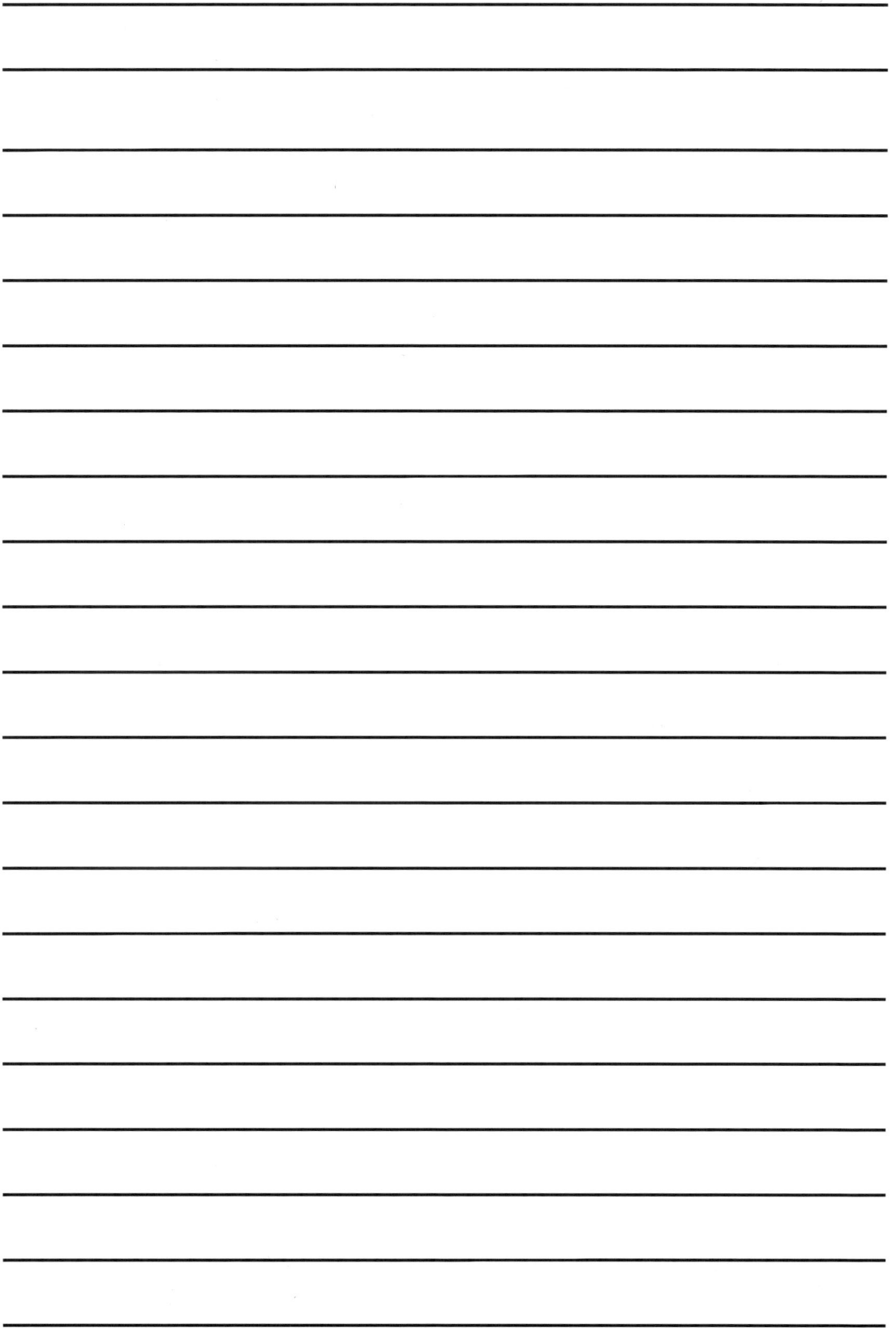

LEGACY

What I believe about procrastination:

_____

_____

_____

_____

_____

_____

_____

_____

_____

_____

_____

_____

_____

_____

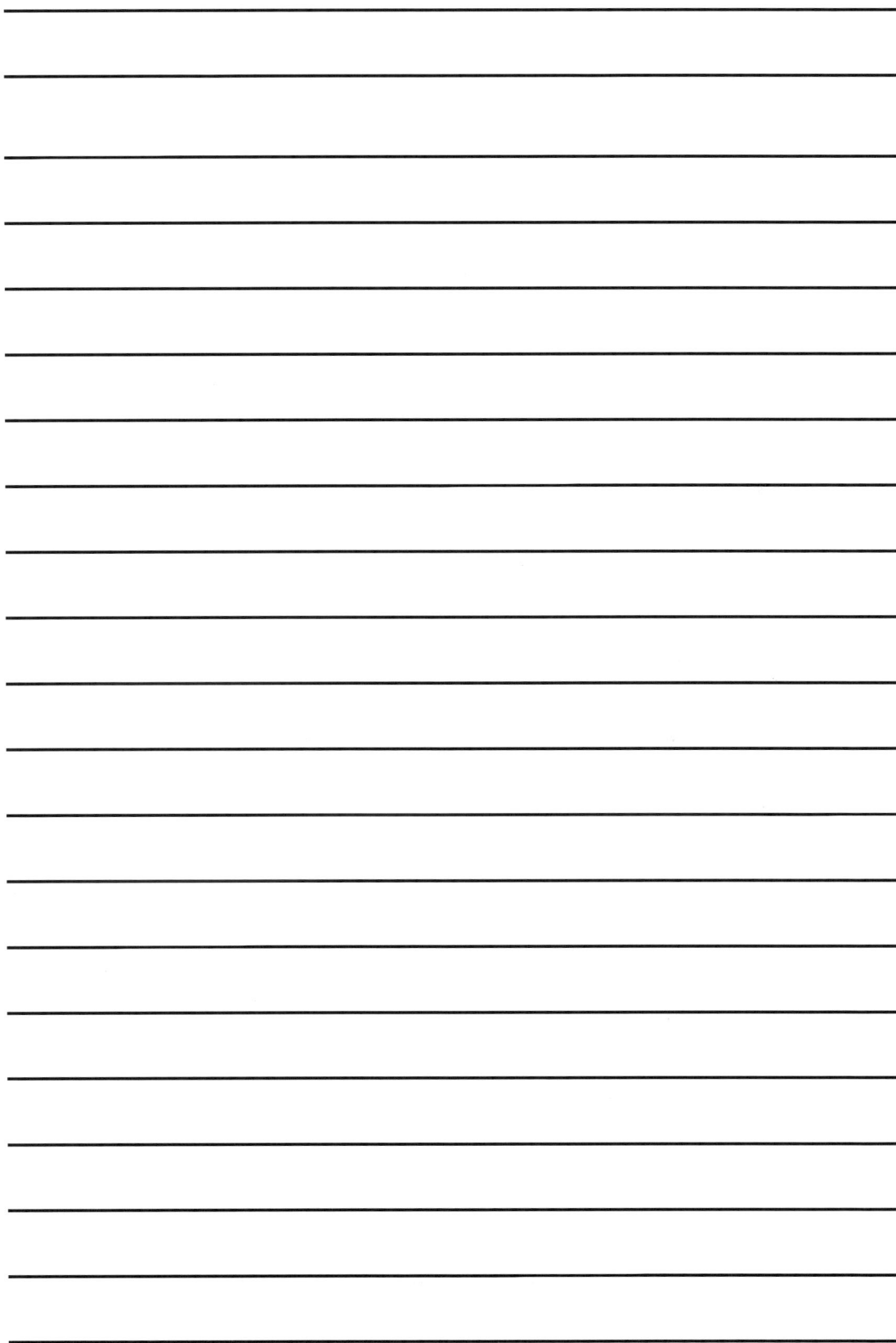

LEGACY

What I believe about pride:

_____

_____

_____

_____

_____

_____

_____

_____

_____

_____

_____

_____

_____

_____

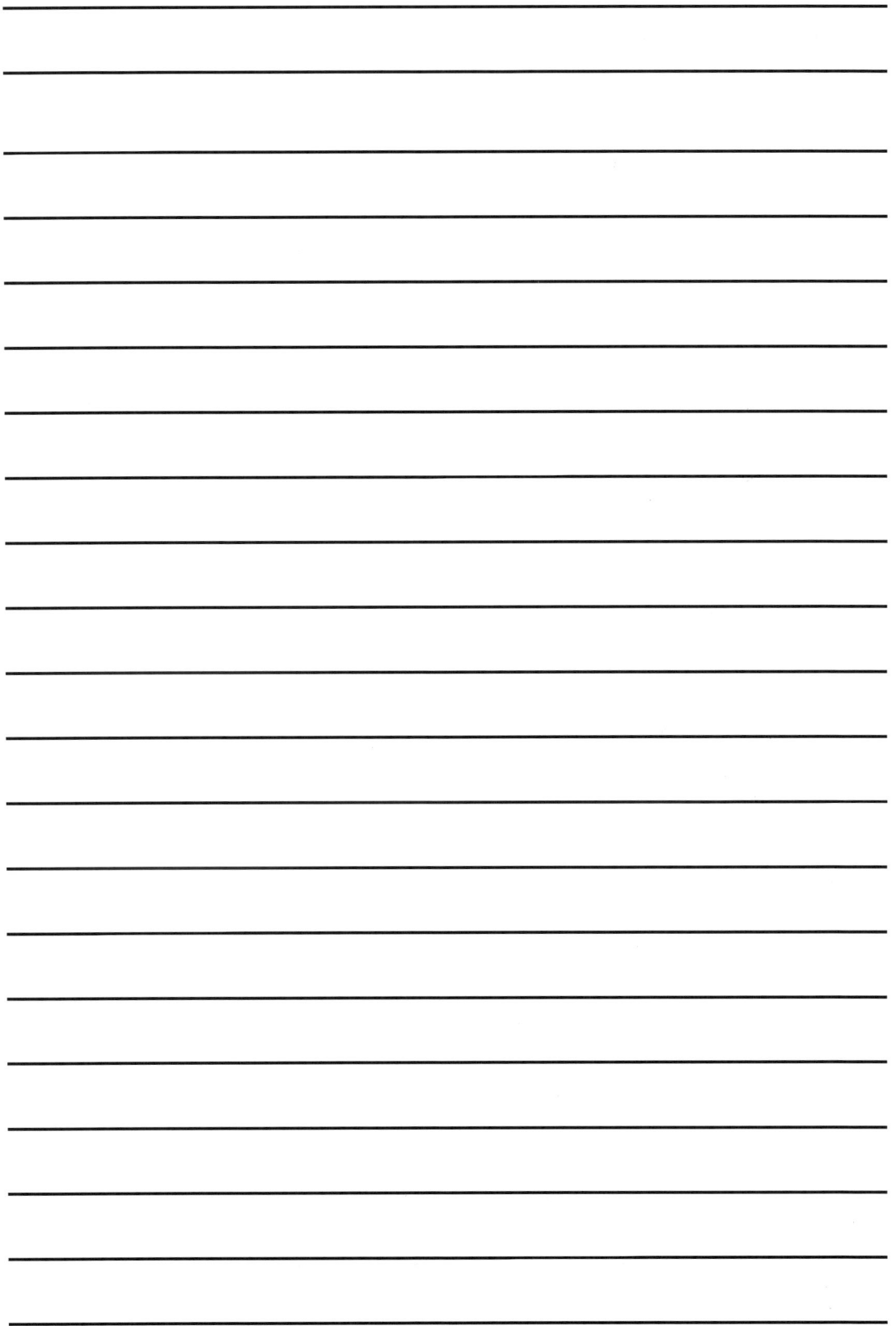

LEGACY

What I believe about being a parent:

_____

_____

_____

_____

_____

_____

_____

_____

_____

_____

_____

_____

_____

_____

_____

_____

_____

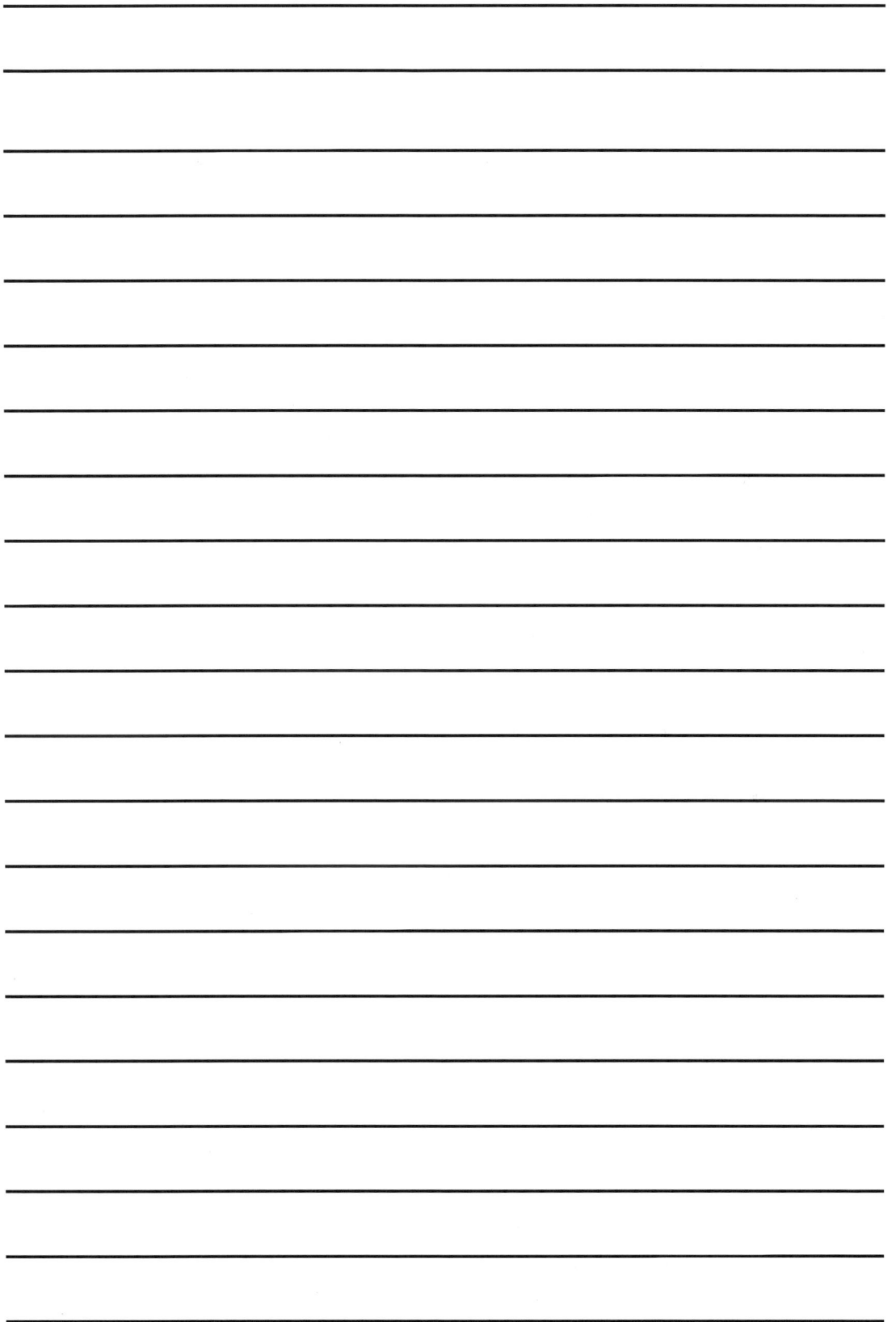

LEGACY

What I believe about time management:

_____

_____

_____

_____

_____

_____

_____

_____

_____

_____

_____

_____

_____

_____

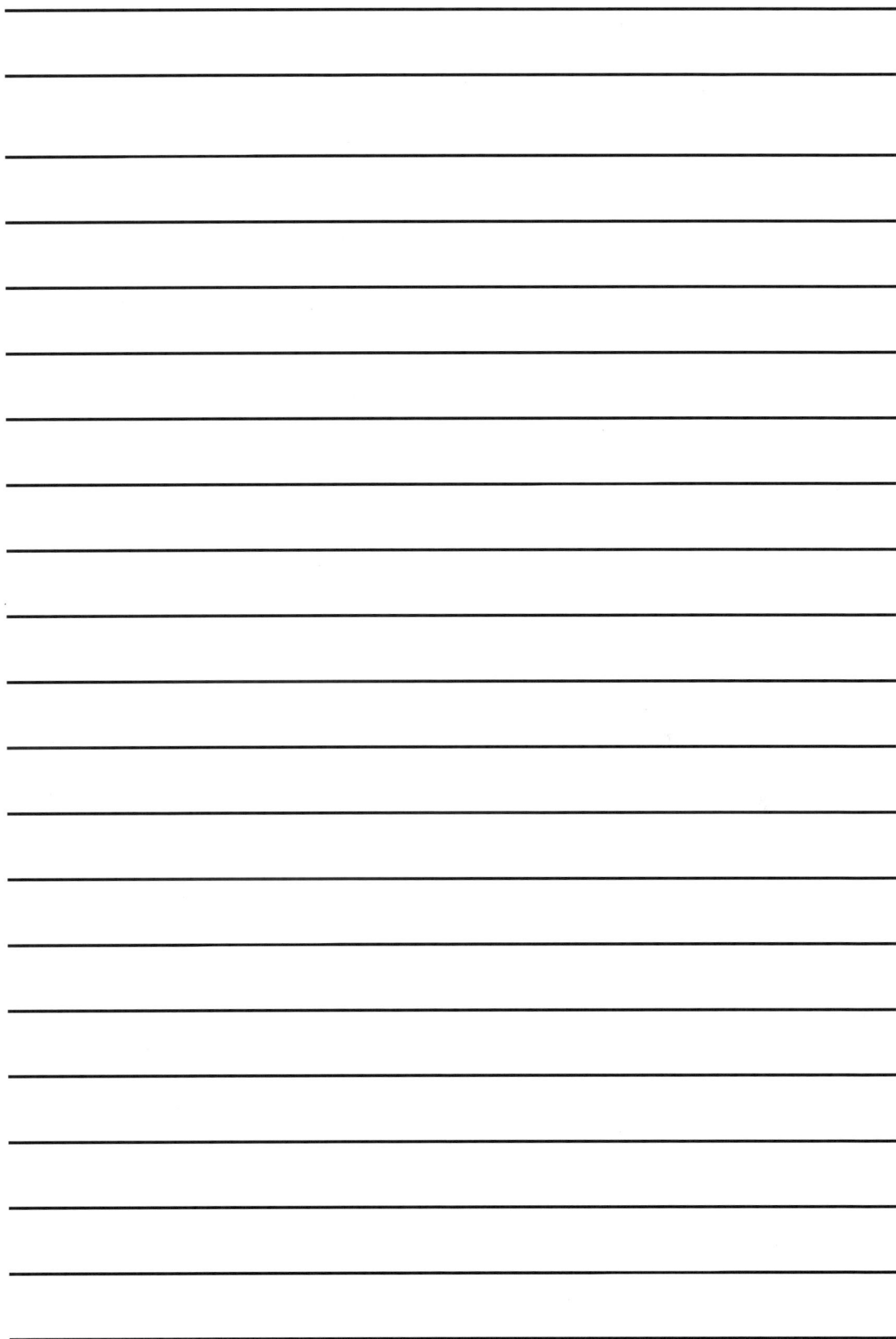

LEGACY

MUST read books:

_____

_____

_____

_____

_____

_____

_____

_____

_____

_____

_____

_____

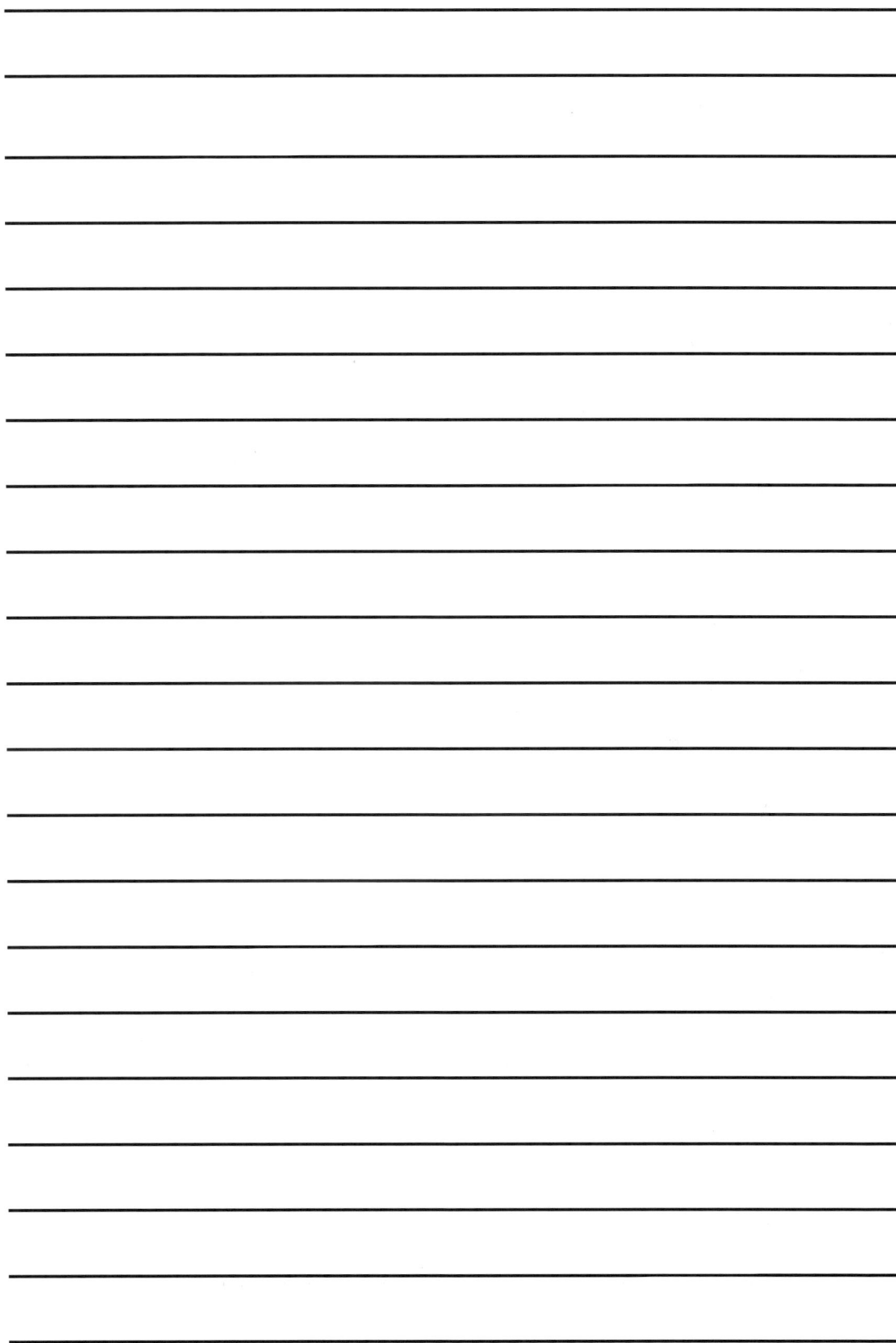

LEGACY

What I believe about anger:

_____

_____

_____

_____

_____

_____

_____

_____

_____

_____

_____

_____

_____

_____

_____

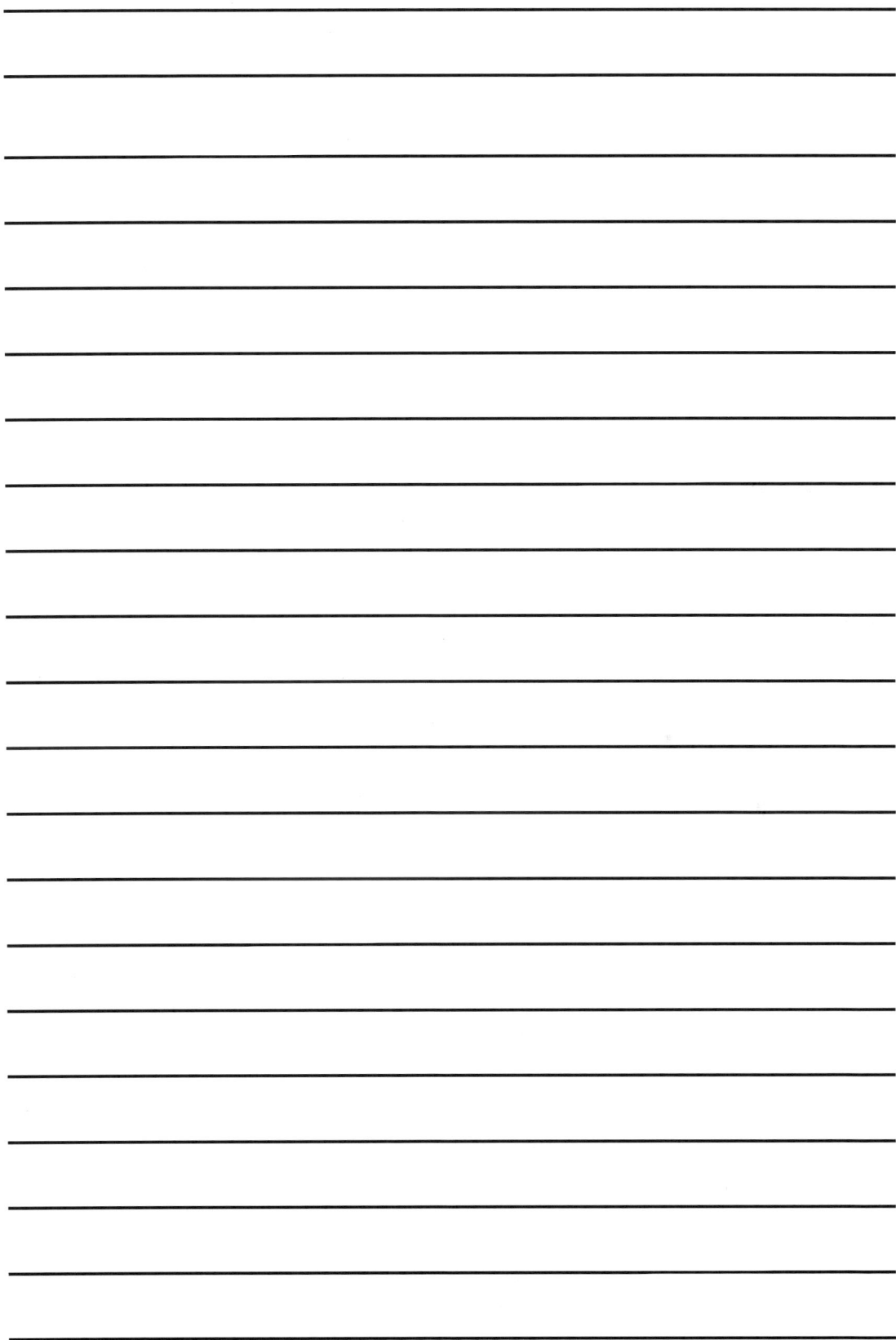

LEGACY

What I believe about tattoos:

_____

_____

_____

_____

_____

_____

_____

_____

_____

_____

_____

_____

_____

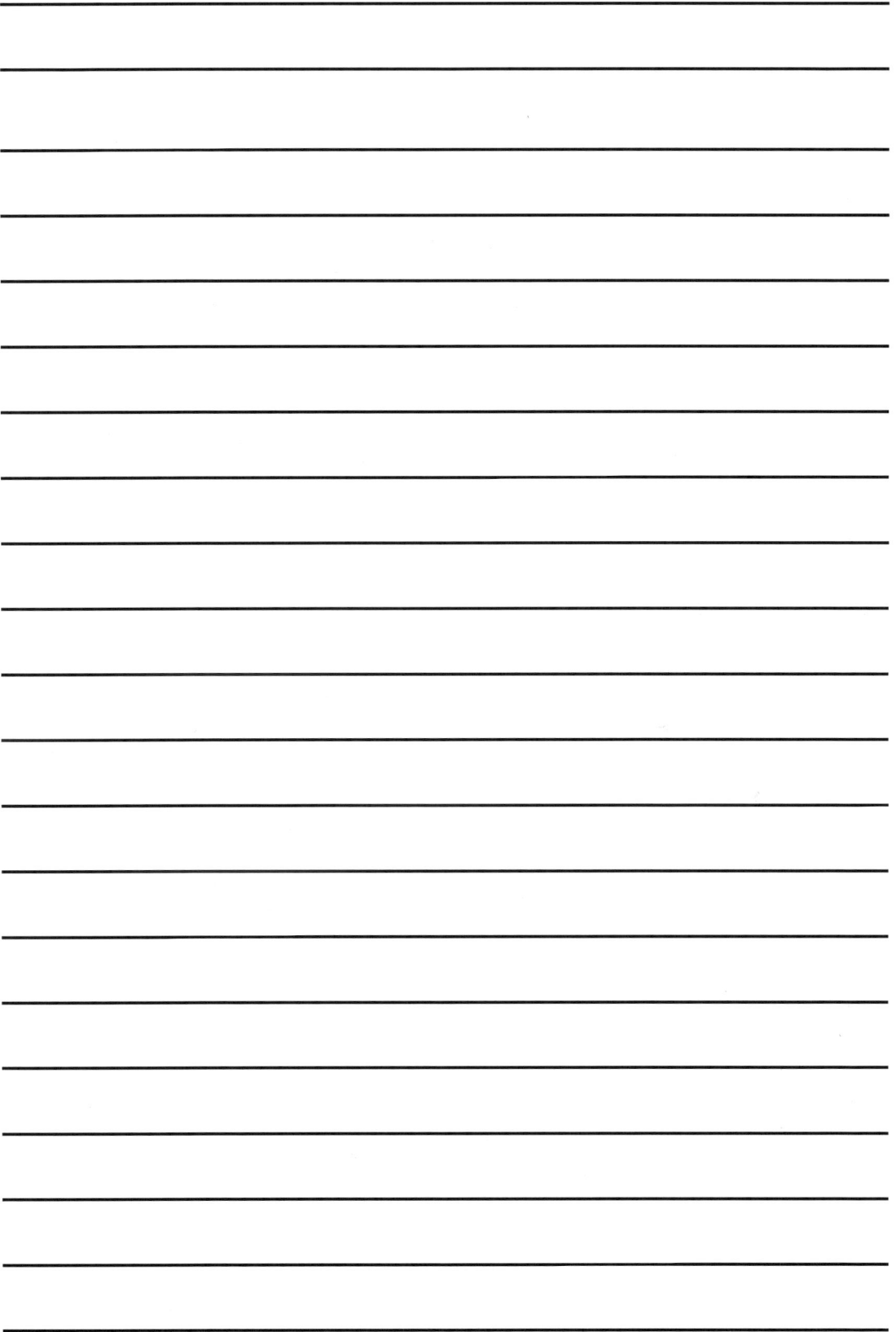

LEGACY

What I believe about humor:

_____

_____

_____

_____

_____

_____

_____

_____

_____

_____

_____

_____

_____

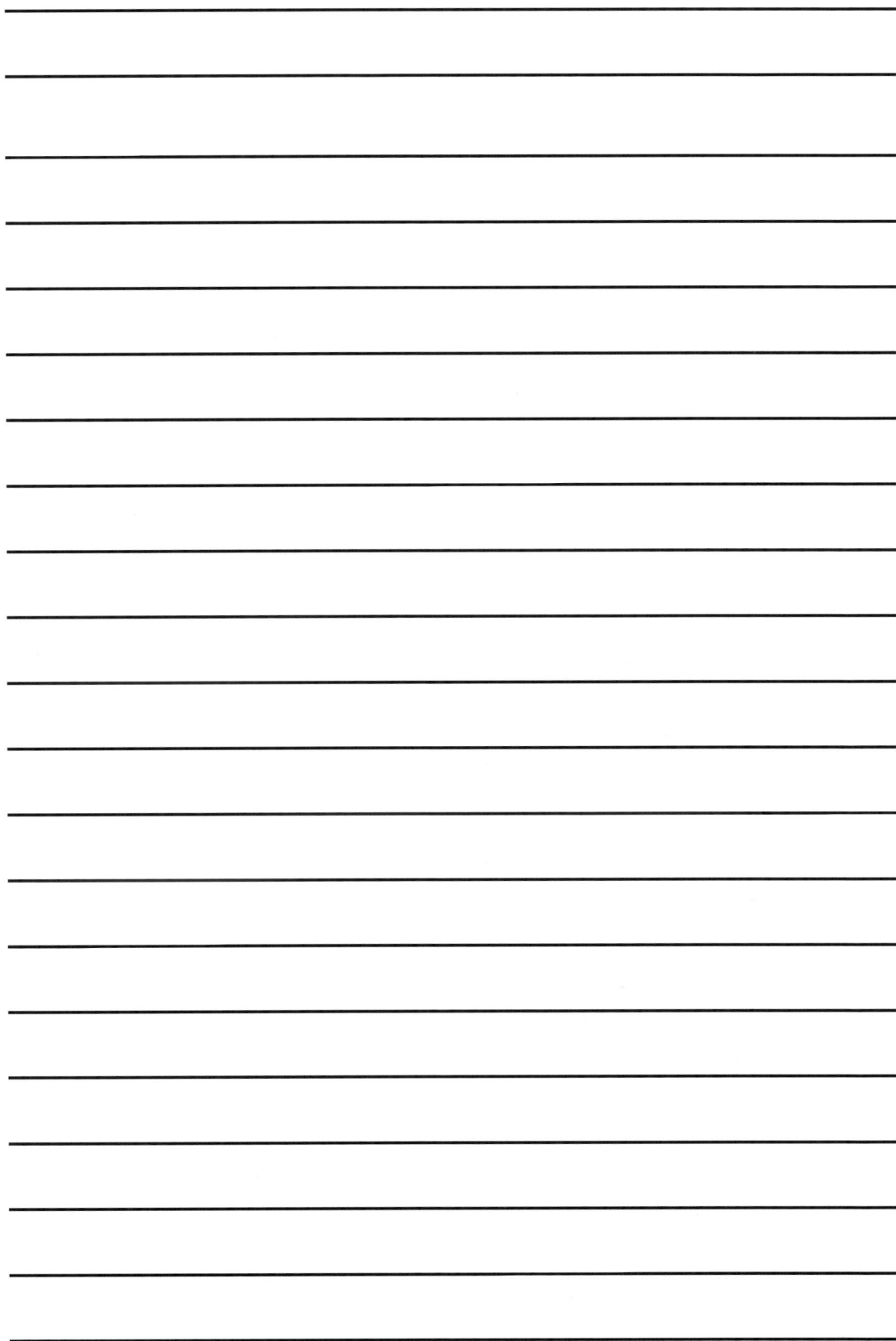

LEGACY

What I believe about thoughts:

_____

_____

_____

_____

_____

_____

_____

_____

_____

_____

_____

_____

_____

_____

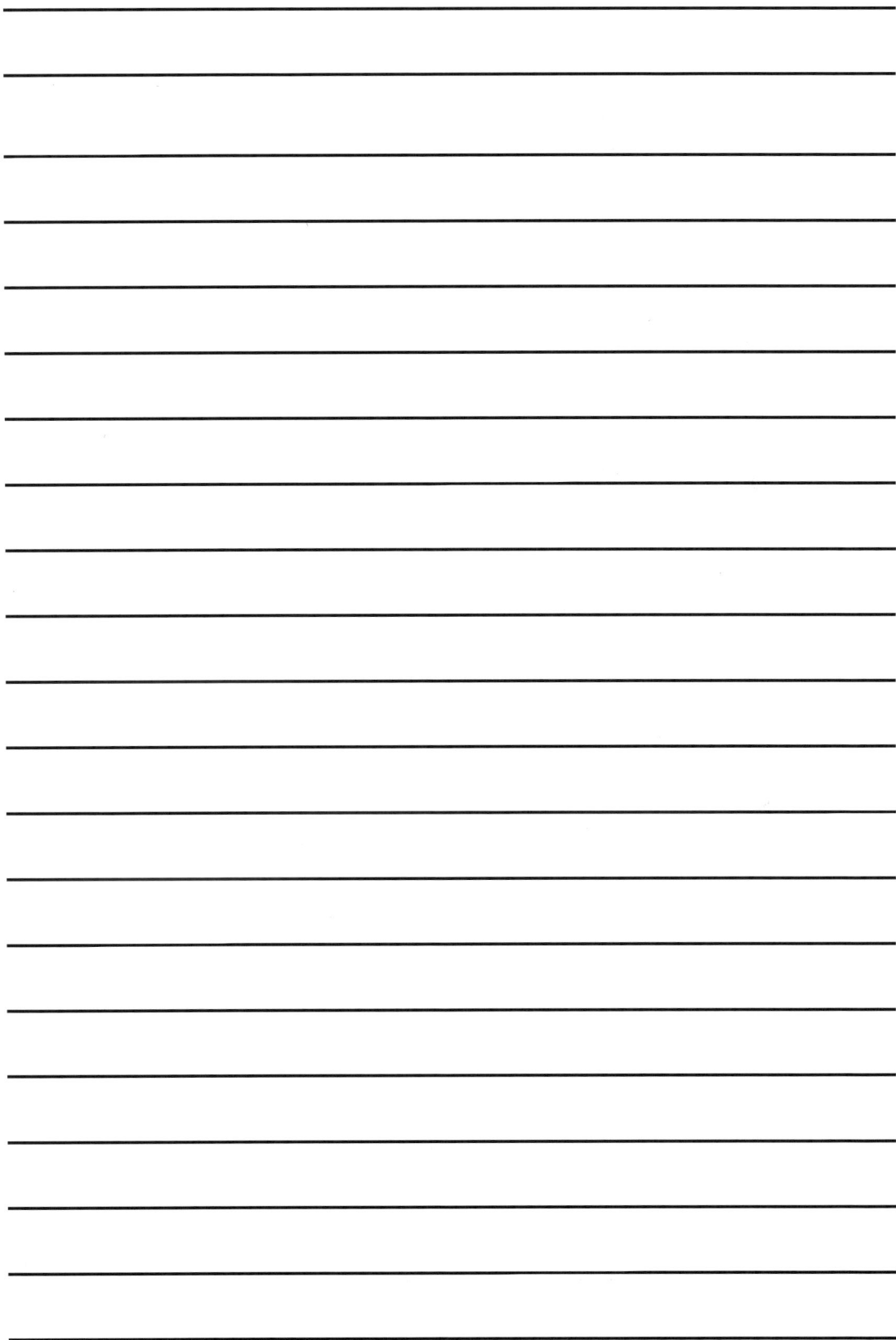

LEGACY

What I believe about gratitude:

_____

_____

_____

_____

_____

_____

_____

_____

_____

_____

_____

_____

_____

_____

_____

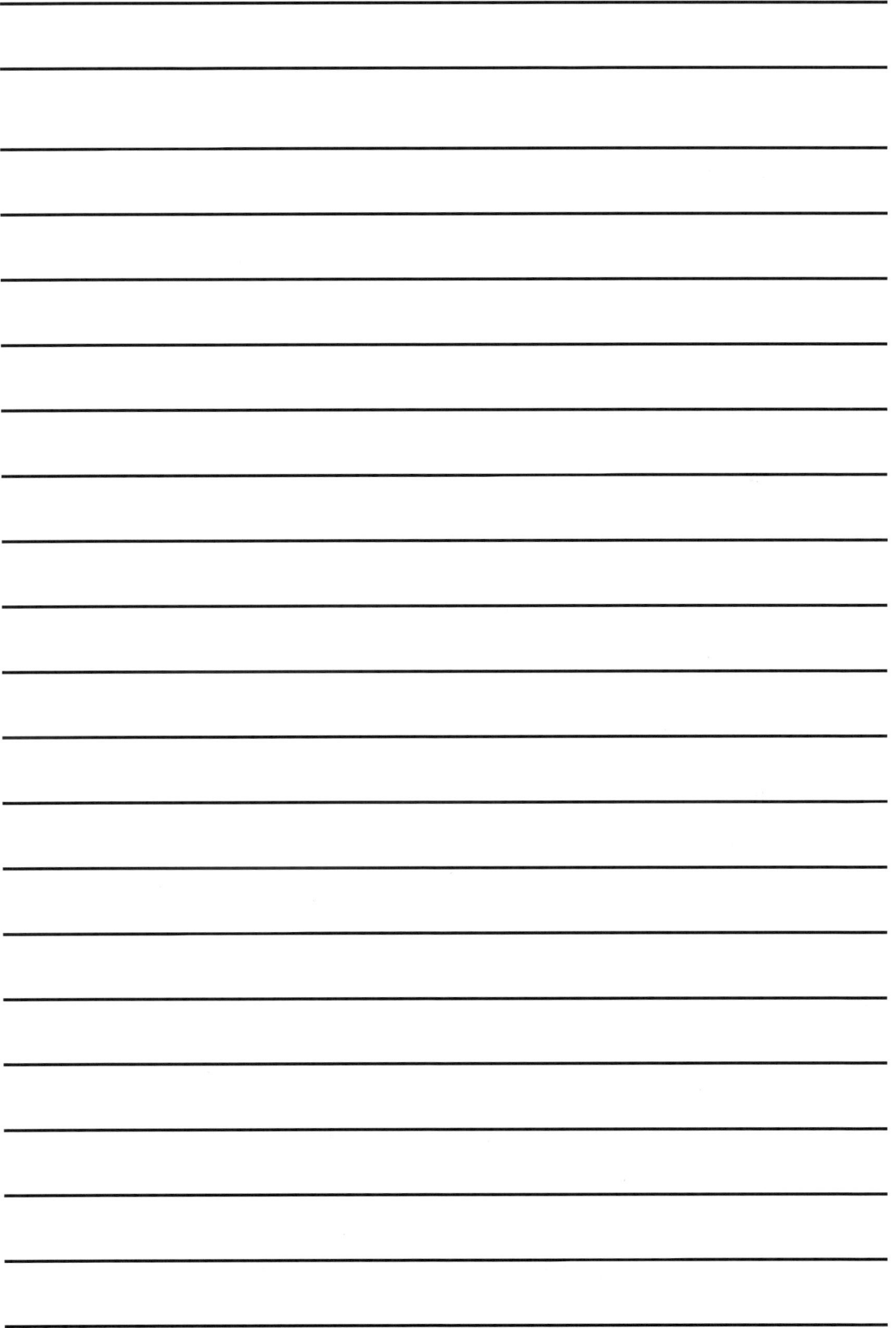

LEGACY

What I believe about insurance:

_____

_____

_____

_____

_____

_____

_____

_____

_____

_____

_____

_____

_____

_____

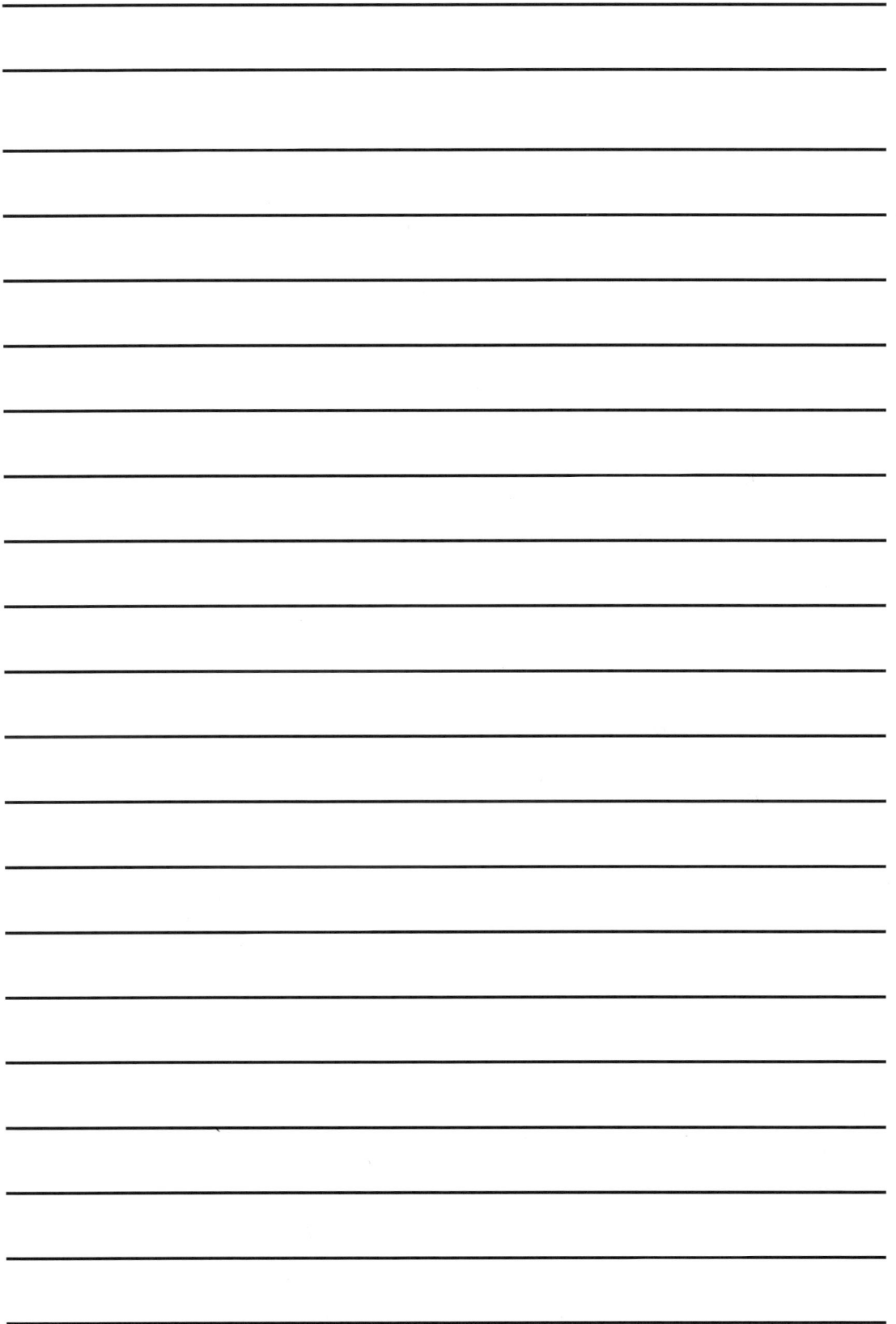

LEGACY

What I believe about being alone and not being lonely:

_____

_____

_____

_____

_____

_____

_____

_____

_____

_____

_____

_____

_____

_____

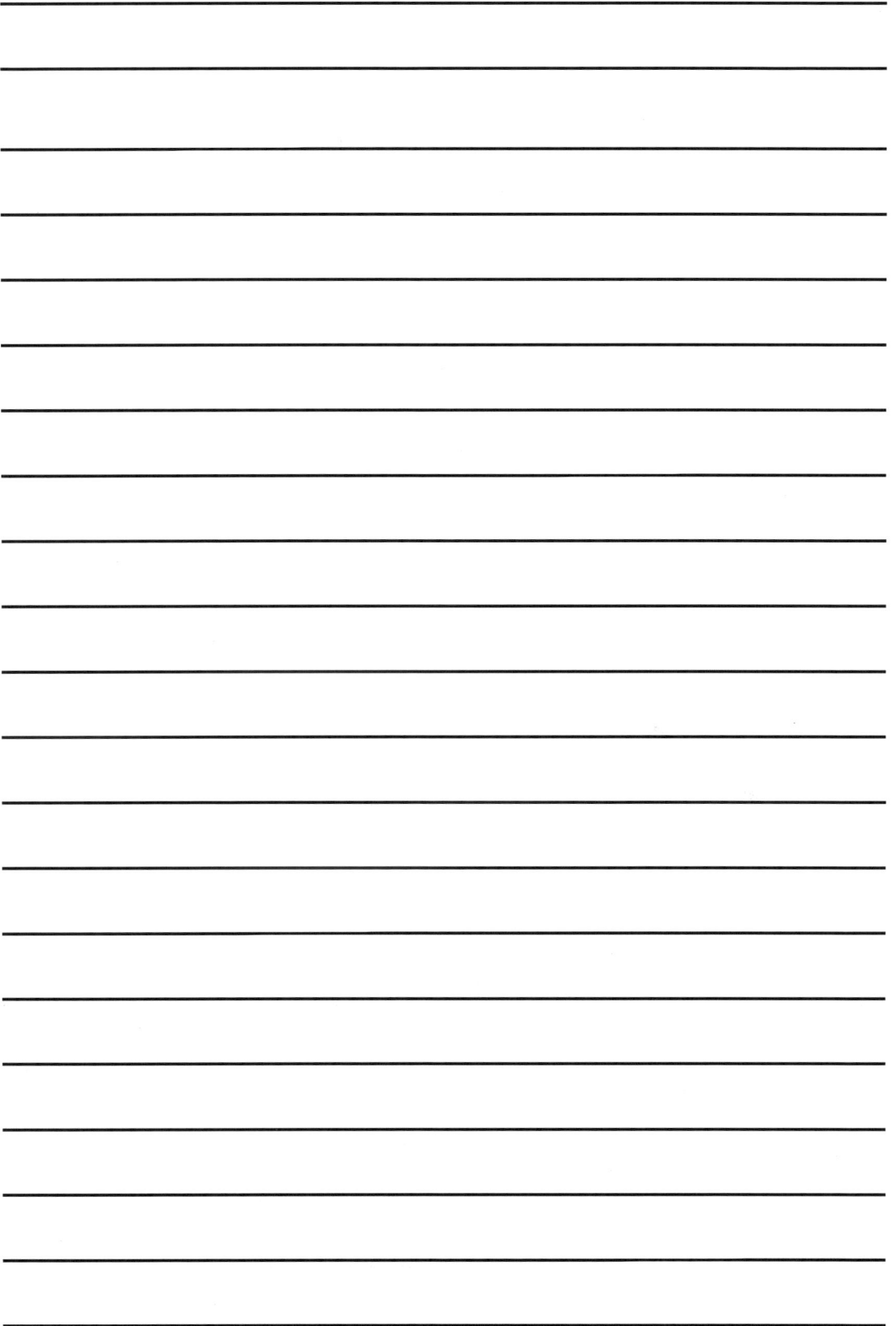

LEGACY

What I believe about self image:

_____

_____

_____

_____

_____

_____

_____

_____

_____

_____

_____

_____

_____

_____

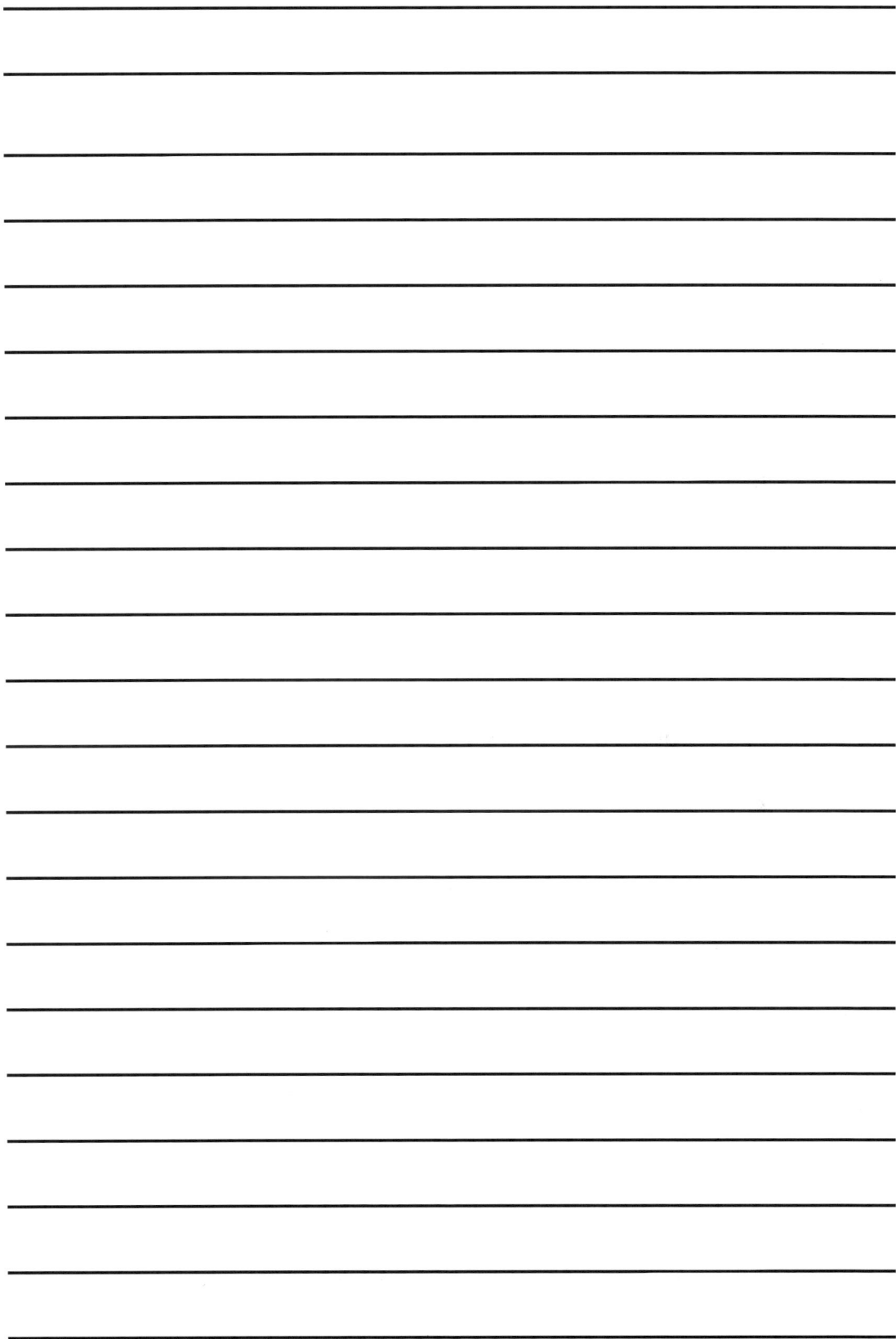

LEGACY

What I believe about mercy:

_____

_____

_____

_____

_____

_____

_____

_____

_____

_____

_____

_____

_____

_____

_____

_____

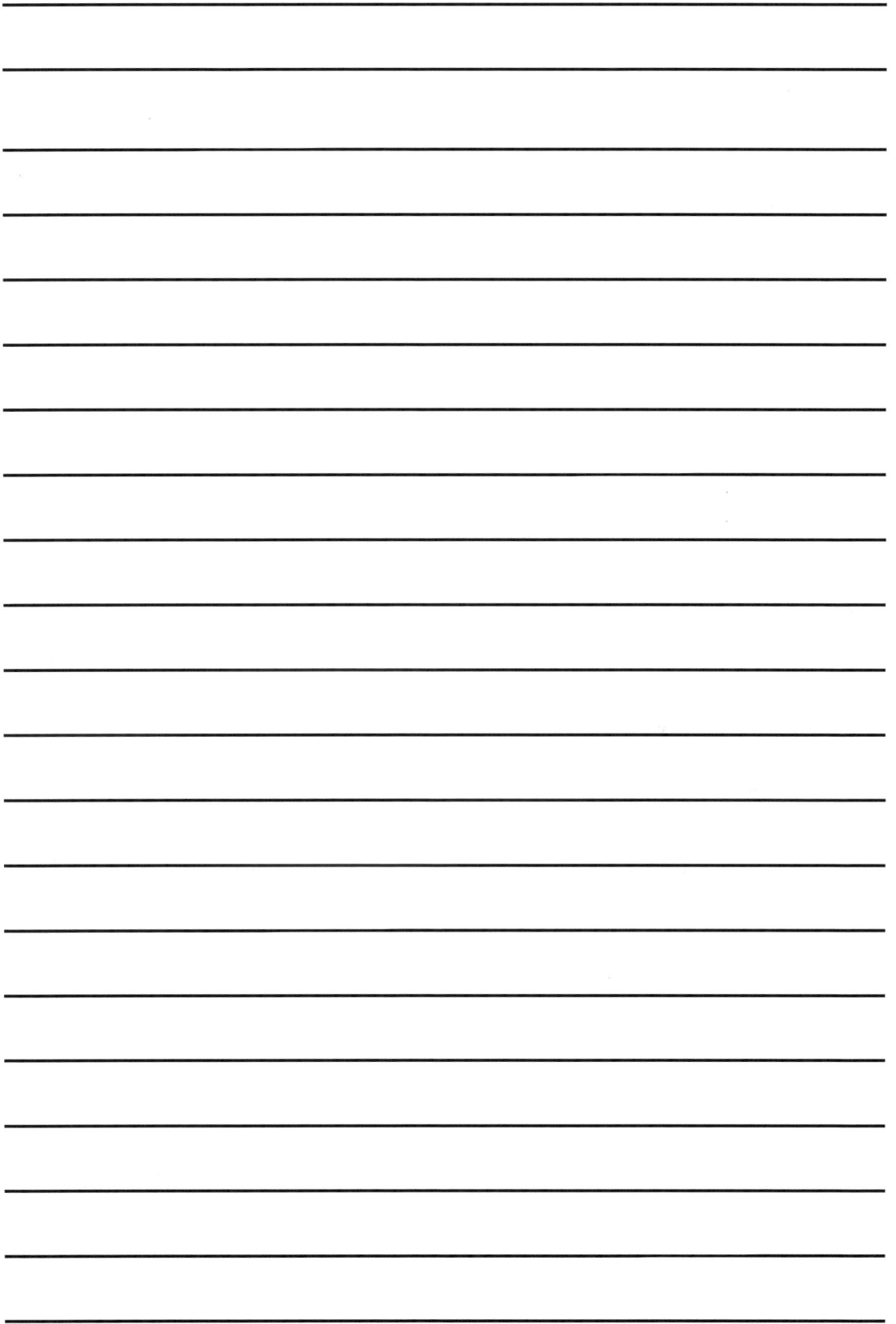

LEGACY

What I believe about obtaining wise counsel:

_____

_____

_____

_____

_____

_____

_____

_____

_____

_____

_____

_____

_____

_____

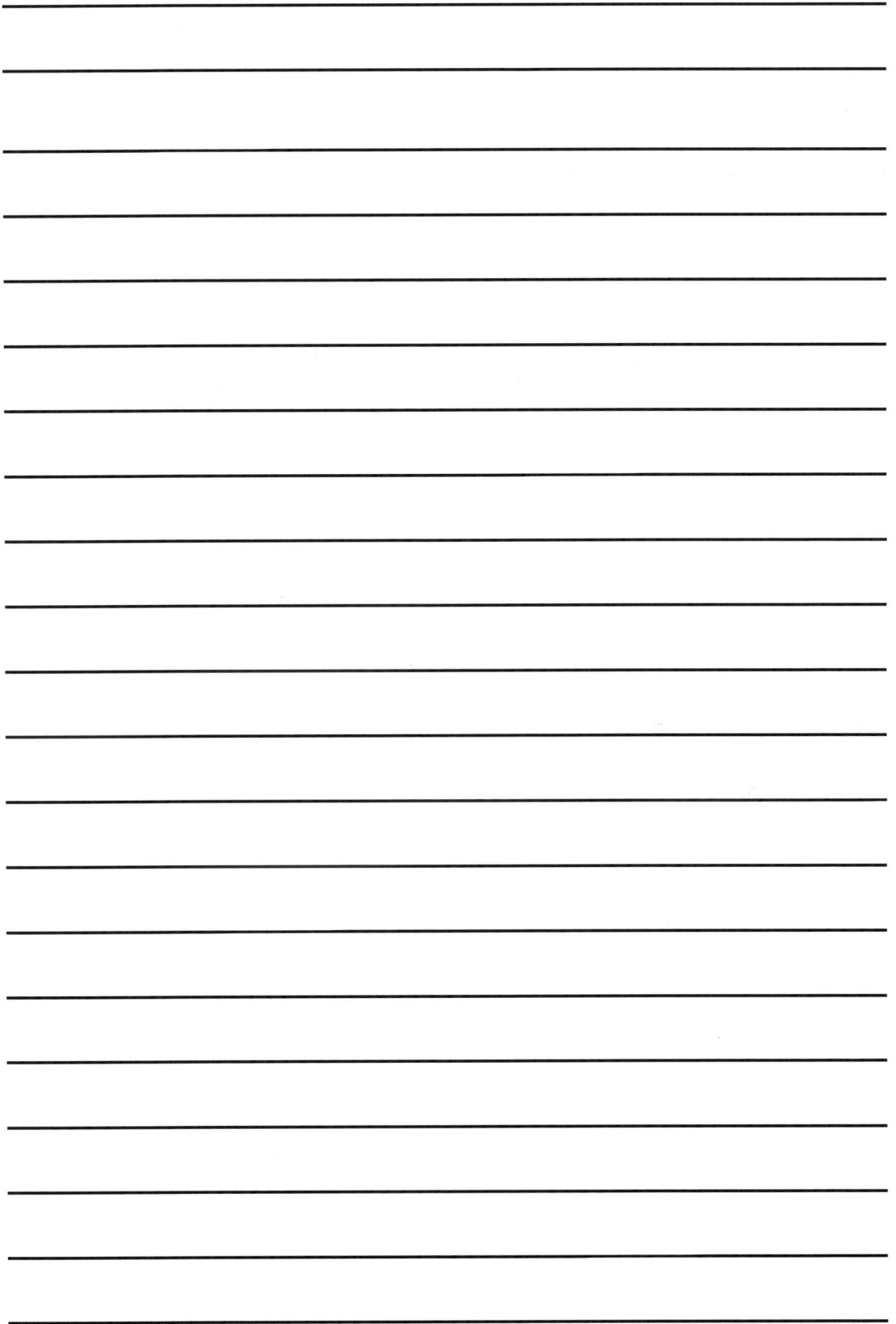

LEGACY

What I believe about finding what you were created to do in life:

_____

_____

_____

_____

_____

_____

_____

_____

_____

_____

_____

_____

_____

_____

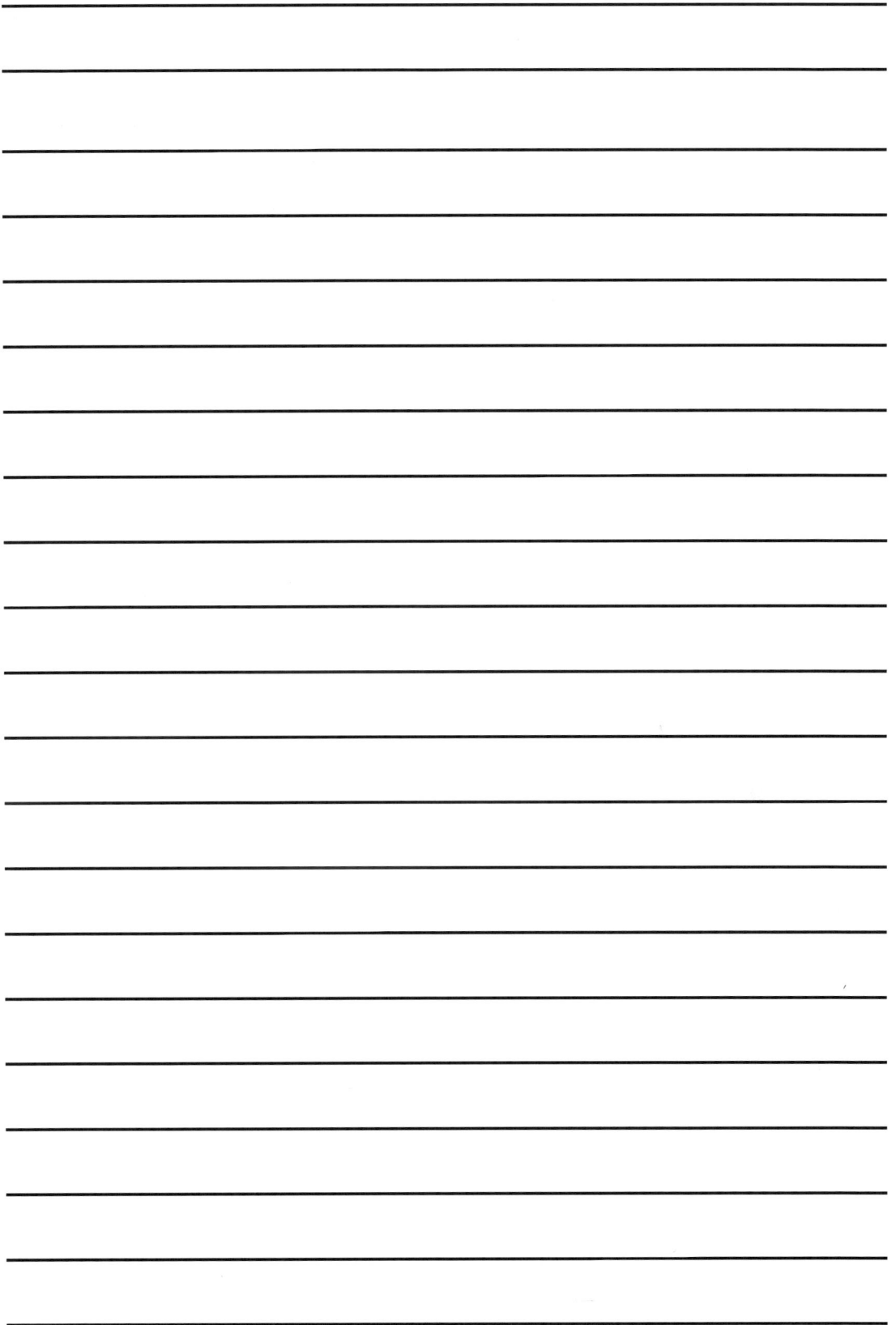

LEGACY

What I believe about going with the flow and being flexible:

_____

_____

_____

_____

_____

_____

_____

_____

_____

_____

_____

_____

_____

_____

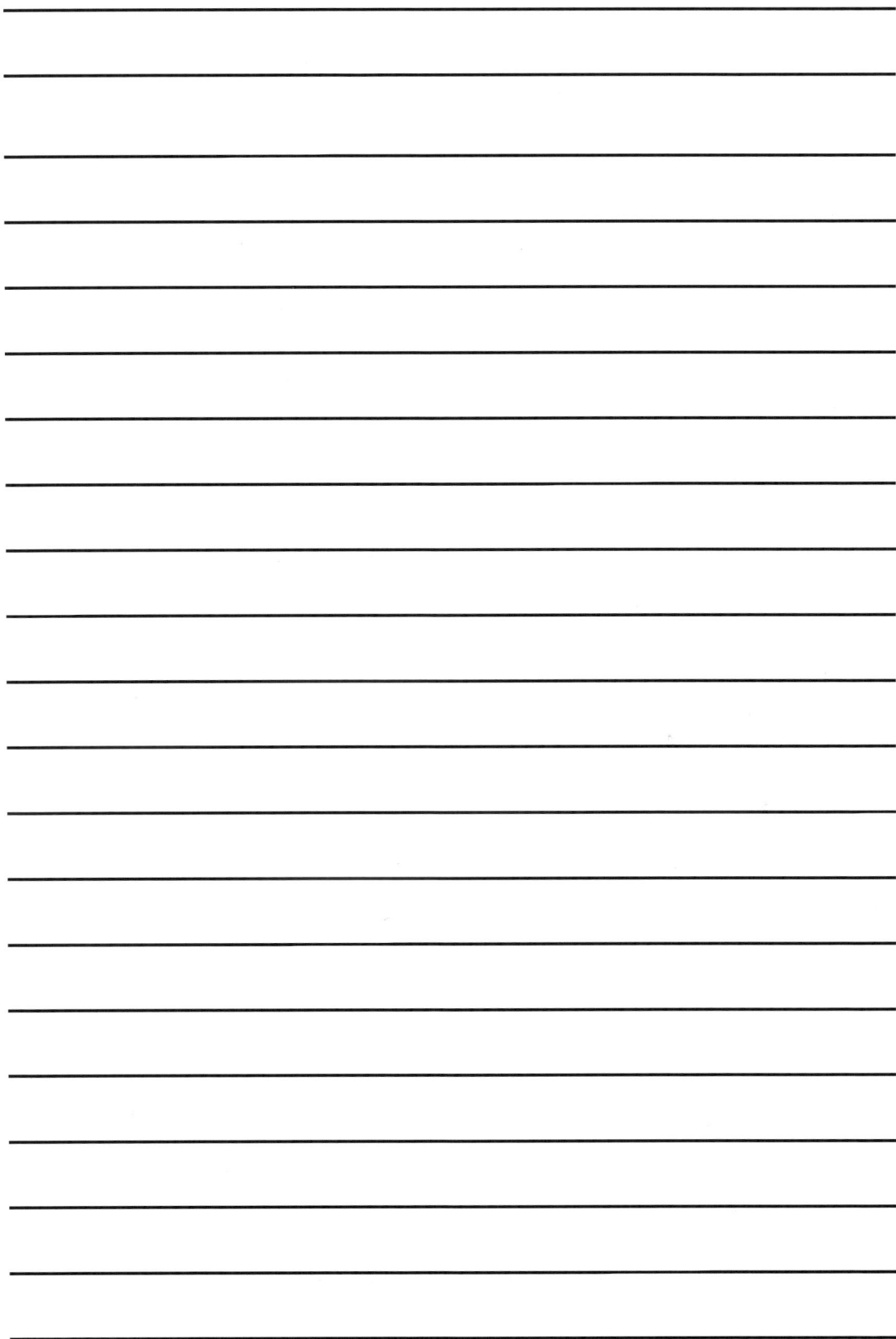

LEGACY

What I believe about lying:

_____

_____

_____

_____

_____

_____

_____

_____

_____

_____

_____

_____

_____

_____

_____

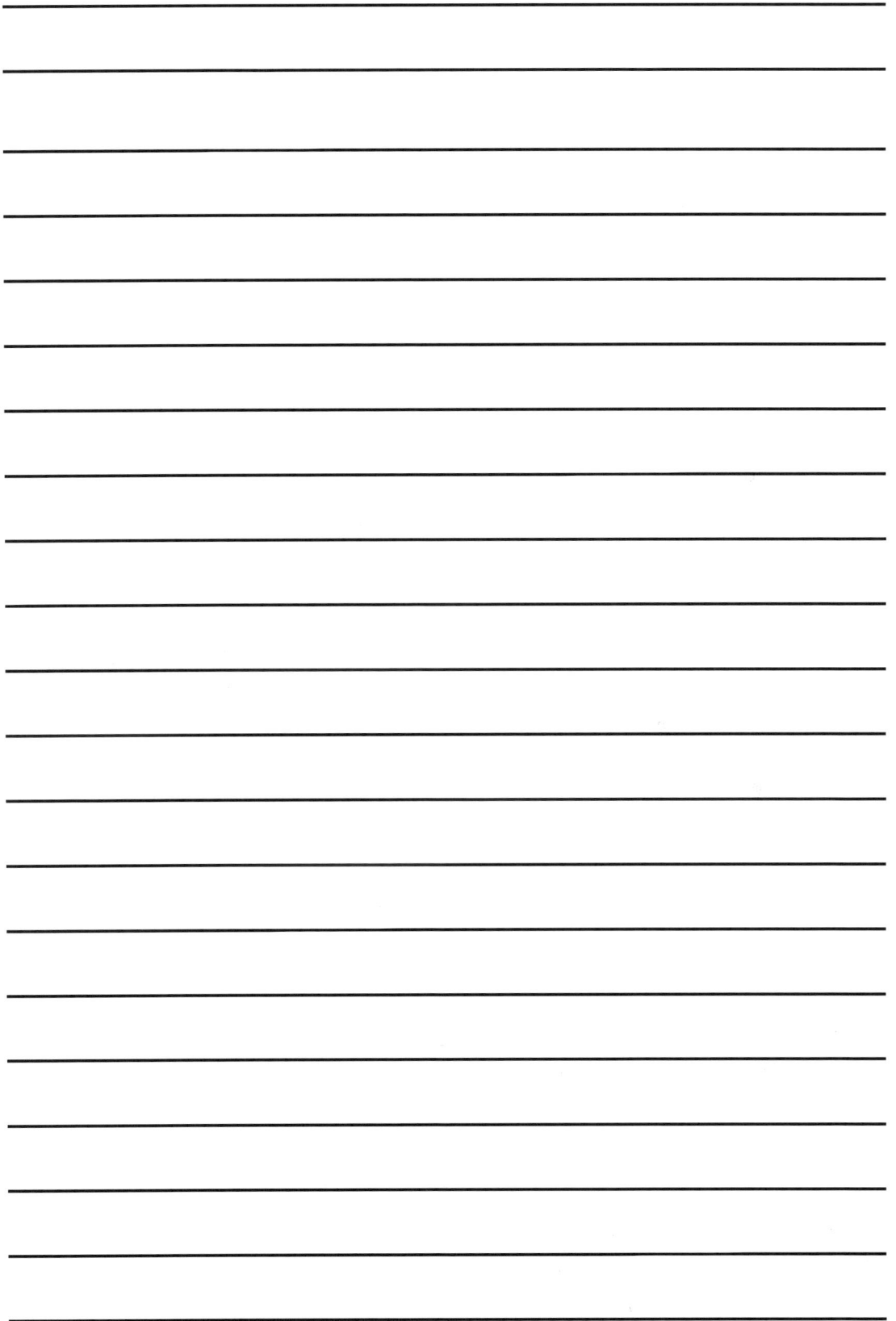

LEGACY

What I believe about giving:

_____

_____

_____

_____

_____

_____

_____

_____

_____

_____

_____

_____

_____

_____

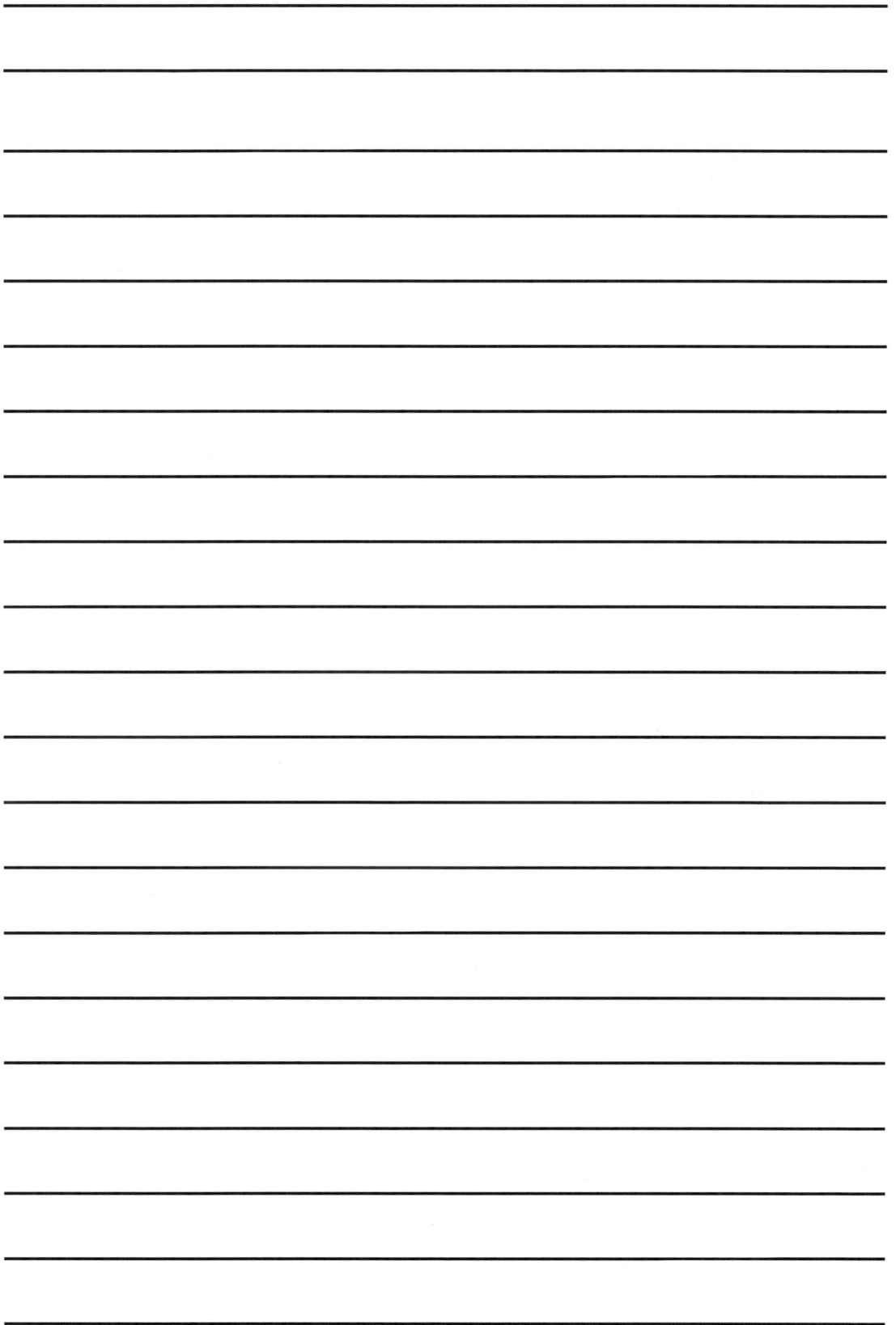

LEGACY

What I believe about trusting your gut:

_____

_____

_____

_____

_____

_____

_____

_____

_____

_____

_____

_____

_____

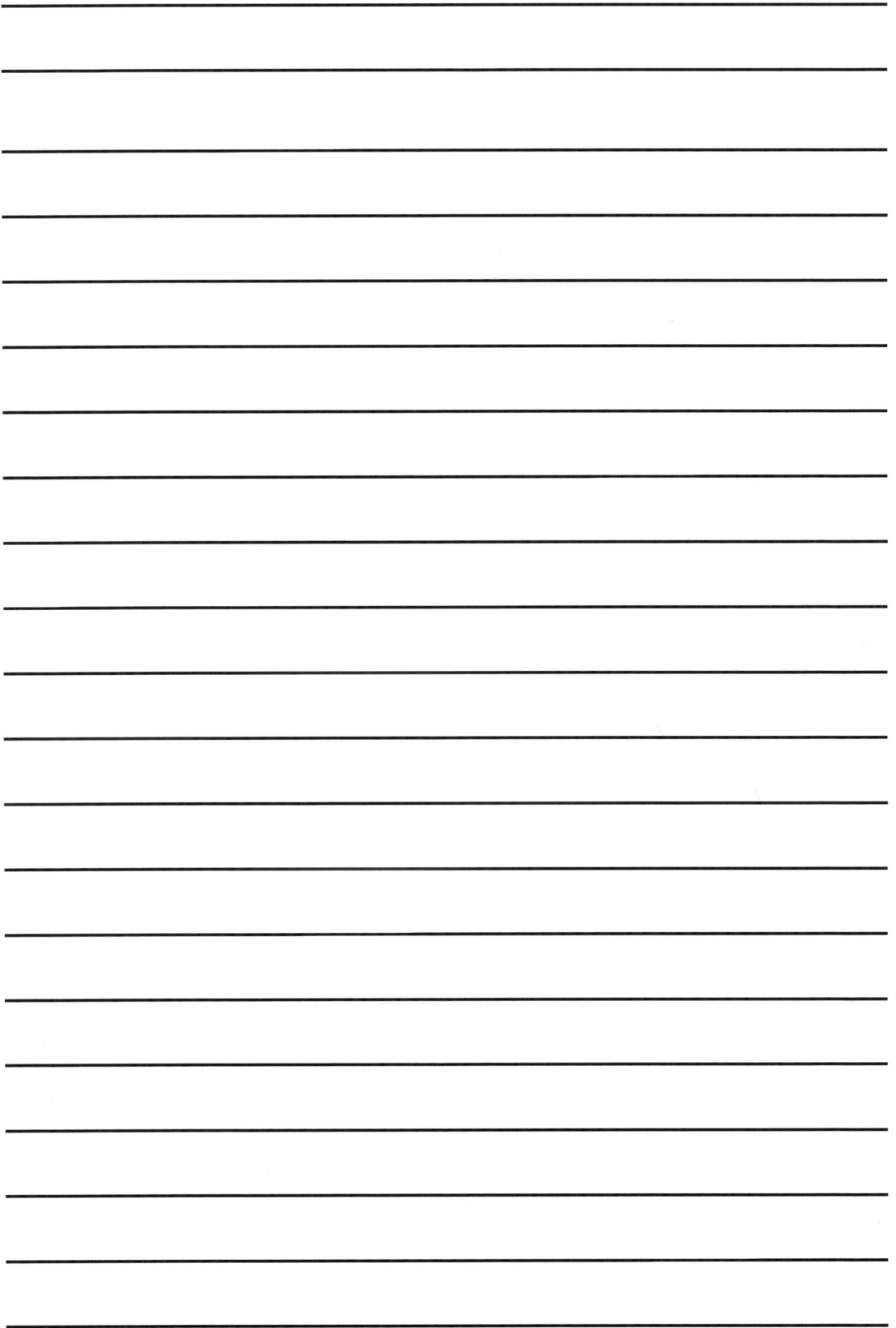

LEGACY

Personal note and final thoughts:

_____

_____

_____

_____

_____

_____

_____

_____

_____

_____

_____

_____

_____

_____

_____

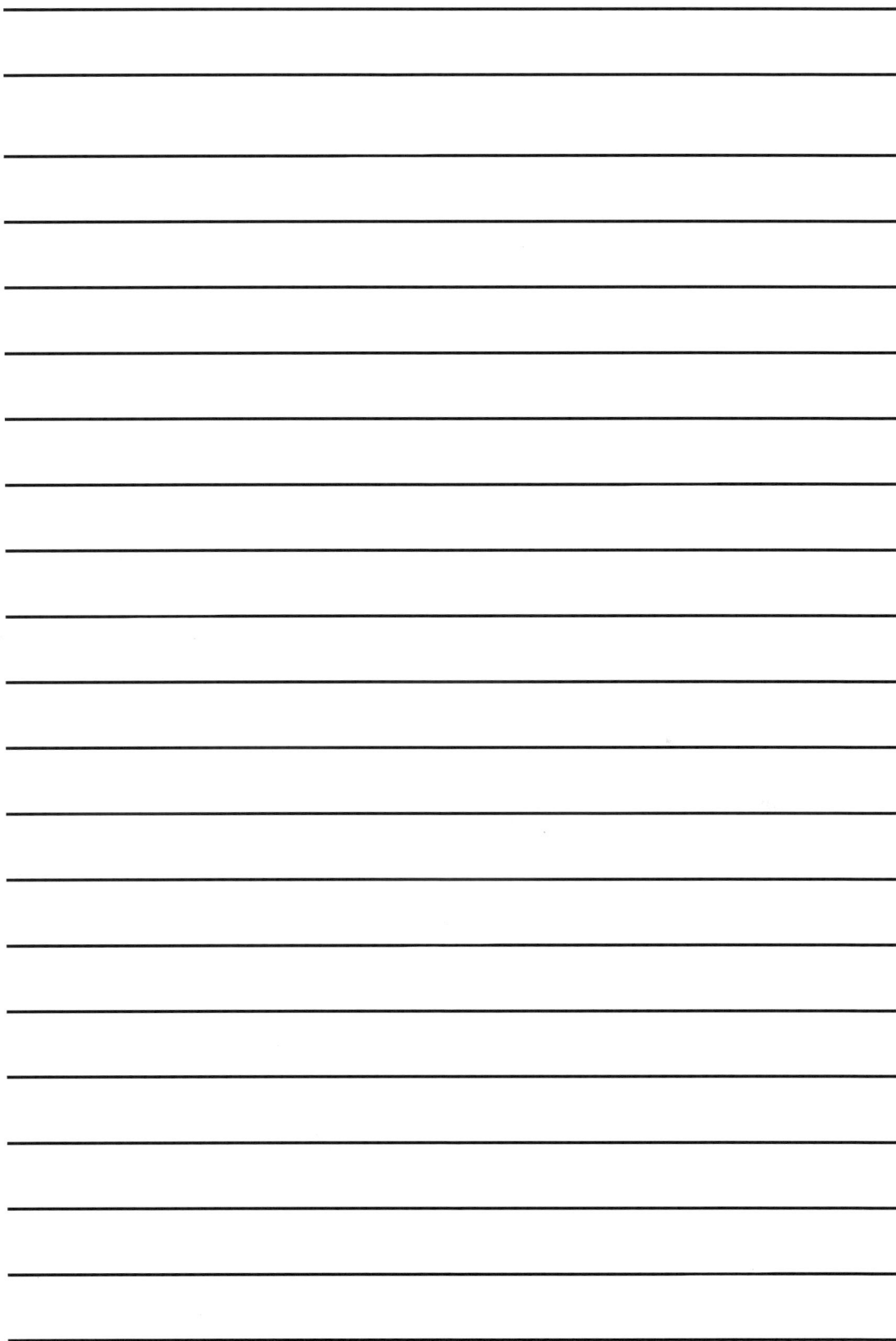

LEGACY

Other books created by SAM Morrison (creativeSAMiam)

- Shining Light into the Darkness
- Praying the Word over your Wounds
- Intentional Acts of Loving-Kindness
- A Year of Proverbs
- Fuel your Body
- Prayer Journal
- A Pondering Place – The Original
- A Pondering Place – Business Version
- A Pondering Place – Scripture Version
- A Pondering Place – 3 in 1

Made in the USA
San Bernardino, CA
21 June 2018